English Echo

Advancing Listening Proficiency with Inspiring Topics

Robert Hickling
Shun Morimoto

NATIONAL
GEOGRAPHIC
LEARNING

Australia · Brazil · Mexico · Singapore · United Kingdom · United States

English Echo—Advancing Listening Proficiency with Inspiring Topics

Robert Hickling / Shun Morimoto

© 2023 Cengage Learning K.K.

Photo Credits:
Cover: © gettyimage; 10: © stock adobe.com; 14: © stock adobe.com; 18: © stock adobe.com;
22: © stock adobe.com; 26: © Fashionstock .com | Dreamstime.com; 27: © stock adobe.com;
30: © GRANGER/ 時事通信フォト , © Artycrafter | Dreamstime.com, © stock adobe.com, © stock adobe.com;
34: © stock adobe.com; 38: © stock adobe.com; 42: © Sports Images | Dreamstime.com;
46: © stock adobe.com; 50: © stock adobe.com; 54: © stock adobe.com, © travelview - stock.adobe.com,
© stock adobe.com, © stock adobe.com; 58: © stock adobe.com; 59: © stock adobe.com,
© Stefan - stock.adobe.com, © Trong Nguyen | Dreamstime.com, © Michael Williams | Dreamstime.com;
62: © stock adobe.com; 66: © stock adobe.com; 67:© stock adobe.com, © stock adobe.com,
© Mistervlad - stock.adobe.com, © stock adobe.com; 70: © stock adobe.com; 74: © stock adobe.com;
78: © stock adobe.com; 82: © Kraximus2010 | Dreamstime.com; 86: © enchanted _fairy | Dreamstime.com,
© Brett Critchley | Dreamstime.com, © stock adobe.com; 90: © stock adobe.com; 94: © stock adobe.com;
98; © stock adobe.com; 102: © stock adobe.com; 106: © stock adobe.com; 110: © stock adobe.com;
114: © stock adobe.com; 118: © stock adobe.com; 122: © stock adobe.com; 126: © stock adobe.com;

For permission to use material from this textbook or product, e-mail to **eltjapan@cengage.com**

ISBN: 978-4-86312-404-2

National Geographic Learning | Cengage Learning K.K.
No. 2 Funato Building 5th Floor
1-11-11 Kudankita, Chiyoda-ku
Tokyo 102-0073
Japan

Tel: 03-3511-4392
Fax: 03-3511-4391

はしがき

　本書は、リスニング力の向上を主軸に据えながら、スピーキング力やライティング力、文法力、語彙・表現力といった力を伸ばすことで、大学生のみなさんが総合的な英語コミュニケーション力を身に付けることを目的としたテキストです。

　本書では、大学生が専攻に関わらず興味・関心をもち、現代社会を生きる上で重要となる 15 のテーマを取り上げます。各 Unit は **Talk with Your Partner** や **Listen to the Dialogue** をはじめとする計 9 セクションから構成されています。**Talk with Your Partner** では、ウォームアップ活動として 2 つの質問についてパートナーと意見を交換することにより、テーマに関する背景知識（スキーマ）を活性化し、学修へのレディネスを高めます。**Listen to the Dialogue** では、テーマに関連した日常会話を聞き、イラストを正しい順番に並べ替える問題 **A** や内容理解問題 **B**、ディクテーション **C** といった活動に取り組みます。**Tips for Listening** では、リスニングを行う上で有益な英語の発音面に関する内容を学修します。ここでは個々の音素や単語の発音に加え、リエゾン（連結）や脱落といった音声変化等を扱いますが、英語音声学の知識がなくても理解できるよう平易な記述を試みました。**Grammar Preview** 及び **Vocabulary Preview** は、続く **Listen to the Short Talk** で出てくる文法項目及び重要語彙を確認し、レディネスを高めることをねらいとしたセクションです。**Grammar Preview** では解説の後に英作文問題に取り組み、**Vocabulary Preview** では空欄補充問題に取り組みます。

　Listen to the Short Talk は、本書のメインとなるセクションです。セクション冒頭に掲載されている写真やイラストを見ながら **Short Talk** を聴き、内容理解問題 **A** に取り組みます。 **B** は **Recap** という名前の通り、**Short Talk** の要約が提示され、空欄に入る正しい語（句）を記入します。 **C** の **Retell** では、**Short Talk** の内容を口頭で再生する活動を行います。**Short Talk** をただ聞くだけでなく、聞いた内容を話したり書いたりしてプロダクションに繋げることによって、リスニング力だけではなくスピーキング力やライティング力の向上を図ることができます。

　続く **Tips for Speaking** では、「相手に共感を求める表現」や「聞き直す時の表現」といった、会話のさまざまな場面で用いられる表現を紹介します。ここで取り扱う表現のほとんどは定型表現（チャンク）であるため、スピーキング活動に即応できるだけでなく、リスニング活動の際にも役立つはずです。**Speak Out** では、**Tips for Speaking** で学修した表現を活用しながら、会話文の完成タスクやペアでのスピーキングタスクに取り組みます。最後の **Useful Vocabulary and Expressions** では、各 Unit のテーマに関連した語彙や表現を紹介します。Unit の最後に学修することも可能ですが、授業前に確認することによって **Speak Out** 等の活動にも活用することができます。

　新型コロナウィルス感染症（COVID-19）をはじめ、学生のみなさんはこれからさまざまな社会的環境の変化に対応することが求められます。その際、英語を使ったコミュニケーション力は必要不可欠です。本書での学びを通して、みなさん一人ひとりが積極的に英語を使ってコミュニケーションを図り、それが共鳴（エコー）し合って新たな時代を切り拓いていく原動力になることを願っています。

著者一同

Table of Contents

Unit		Title
Unit 1		Digital Detox
Unit 2		The Sharing Economy
Unit 3		Clothes & Fashion
Unit 4		What Is Animal Intelligence?
Unit 5		The Power of Grit
Unit 6		Telework
Unit 7		Smart Cities
Unit 8		Historical Sites
Unit 9		Sports & the Brain
Unit 10		Poetic Justice
Unit 11		The Magic of Hot Springs
Unit 12		Living with Less
Unit 13		Street Food
Unit 14		Going Cashless
Unit 15		English as a Global Language

5

本書の構成と使い方

各 Unit は 8 ページ構成です。以下に、それぞれの項目やアクティビティの目的と使い方を説明します。

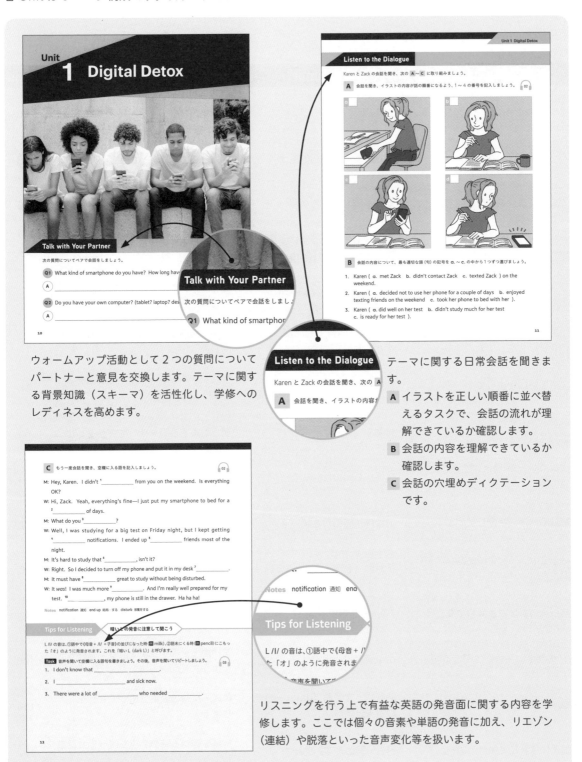

ウォームアップ活動として 2 つの質問について
パートナーと意見を交換します。テーマに関す
る背景知識（スキーマ）を活性化し、学修への
レディネスを高めます。

テーマに関する日常会話を聞きま
す。

A イラストを正しい順番に並べ替
えるタスクで、会話の流れが理
解できているか確認します。

B 会話の内容を理解できているか
確認します。

C 会話の穴埋めディクテーション
です。

リスニングを行う上で有益な英語の発音面に関する内容を学
修します。ここでは個々の音素や単語の発音に加え、リエゾン
（連結）や脱落といった音声変化等を扱います。

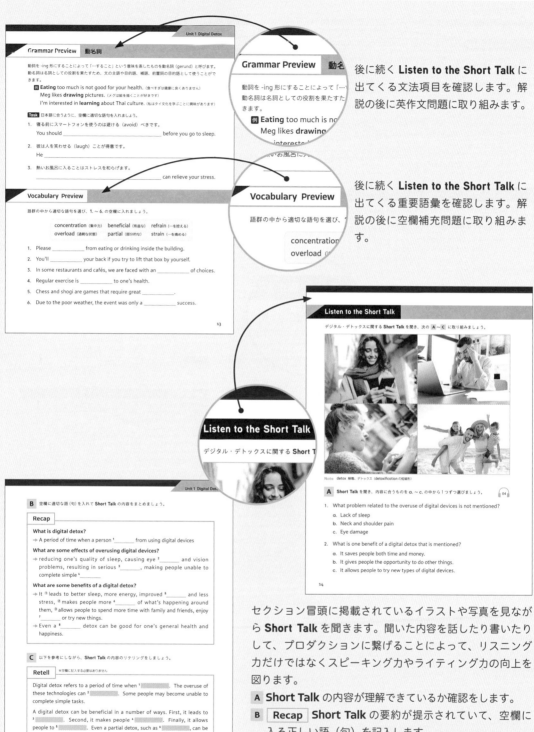

後に続く **Listen to the Short Talk** に出てくる文法項目を確認します。解説の後に英作文問題に取り組みます。

後に続く **Listen to the Short Talk** に出てくる重要語彙を確認します。解説の後に空欄補充問題に取り組みます。

セクション冒頭に掲載されているイラストや写真を見ながら **Short Talk** を聞きます。聞いた内容を話したり書いたりして、プロダクションに繋げることによって、リスニング力だけではなくスピーキング力やライティング力の向上を図ります。

A **Short Talk** の内容が理解できているか確認をします。

B Recap **Short Talk** の要約が提示されていて、空欄に入る正しい語（句）を記入します。

C Retell **Short Talk** の内容を口頭で再生する活動を行います。スクリプトをそのまま再現するのではなく、内容を伝えることをめざしましょう。

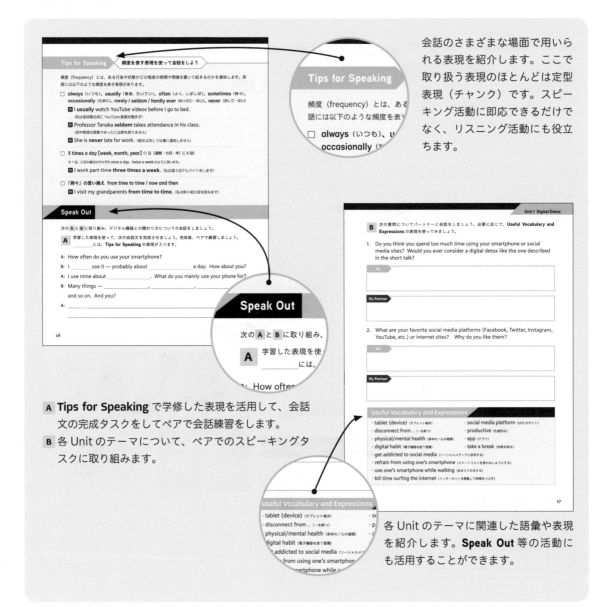

会話のさまざまな場面で用いられる表現を紹介します。ここで取り扱う表現のほとんどは定型表現（チャンク）です。スピーキング活動に即応できるだけでなく、リスニング活動にも役立ちます。

Ⓐ **Tips for Speaking** で学修した表現を活用して、会話文の完成タスクをしてペアで会話練習をします。
Ⓑ 各 Unit のテーマについて、ペアでのスピーキングタスクに取り組みます。

各 Unit のテーマに関連した語彙や表現を紹介します。**Speak Out** 等の活動にも活用することができます。

Tips for Speaking 頻度を表す表現を使って会話をしよう

頻度 (frequency) とは、ある行為や状態がどの程度の期間や間隔を置いて起きるのかを意味します。英語には以下のような頻度を表す表現があります。

☐ **always**（いつも）、**usually**（普段、たいてい）、**often**（よく、しばしば）、**sometimes**（時々）、**occasionally**（たまに）、**rarely / seldom / hardly ever**（めったに…ない）、**never**（決して…ない）
   Ⓔ I **usually** watch YouTube videos before I go to bed.
   （私は普段寝る前に YouTube 動画を観ます）
   Ⓔ Professor Tanaka **seldom** takes attendance in his class.
   （田中教授は授業でめったに出席を取りません）
   Ⓔ She is **never** late for work.（彼女は決して仕事に遅刻しません）

☐ **X times a day [week, month, year]**（1日［週間・カ月・年］に X 回）
   ※1回、2回の場合はそれぞれ once a day、twice a week のように言います。
   Ⓔ I work part-time **three times a week**.（私は週3回アルバイトをします）

☐「時々」の言い換え **from time to time / now and then**
   Ⓔ I visit my grandparents **from time to time**.（私は時々祖父母を訪ねます）

Speak Out

次の Ⓐ と Ⓑ に取り組み、デジタル機器との関わり方についての会話をしましょう。

Ⓐ 学習した表現を使って、次の会話文を完成させましょう。完成後、ペアで練習しましょう。
　　_____ には、**Tips for Speaking** の表現が入ります。

A: How often do you use your smartphone?
B: I _____ use it — probably about _____ a day. How about you?
A: I use mine about _____ . What do you mainly use your phone for?
B: Many things — _____ , _____ , _____
   and so on. And you?
A: _____
   _____

16

Unit 1 Digital Detox

Ⓑ 次の質問についてパートナーと会話をしましょう。必要に応じて、**Useful Vocabulary and Expressions** の表現を使ってみましょう。

1. Do you think you spend too much time using your smartphone or social media sites? Would you ever consider a digital detox like the one described in the short talk?

   Me

   My Partner

2. What are your favorite social media platforms (Facebook, Twitter, Instagram, YouTube, etc.) or internet sites? Why do you like them?

   Me

   My Partner

Useful Vocabulary and Expressions

- tablet (device)（タブレット端末）
- disconnect from ...（…を断つ）
- physical/mental health（身体の／心の健康）
- digital habit（電子機器を使う習慣）
- get addicted to social media（ソーシャルメディアに依存する）
- refrain from using one's smartphone（スマートフォンを使わないようにする）
- use one's smartphone while walking（歩きスマホをする）
- kill time surfing the internet（インターネットを閲覧して時間をつぶす）

- social media platform（SNS のサイト）
- productive（生産的な）
- app（アプリ）
- take a break（休憩を取る）

17

8

音声ファイルの利用方法

 のアイコンがある箇所の音声ファイルにアクセスできます。

https://ngljapan.com/egecho-audio/

❶ 上記の URL にアクセス、または QR コードをスマートフォンなどのリーダーでスキャン

❷ 表示されるファイル名をクリックして音声ファイルをダウンロードまたは再生

1 Digital Detox

Talk with Your Partner

次の質問についてペアで会話をしましょう。

Q1 What kind of smartphone do you have? How long have you had it?

A _____

Q2 Do you have your own computer? (tablet? laptop? desktop?)

A _____

Listen to the Dialogue

Karen と Zack の会話を聞き、次の A ～ C に取り組みましょう。

A 会話を聞き、イラストの内容が話の順番になるよう、1 ～ 4 の番号を記入しましょう。

B 会話の内容について、最も適切な語 (句) の記号を a. ～ c. の中から 1 つずつ選びましょう。

1. Karen (a. met Zack b. didn't contact Zack c. texted Zack) on the weekend.

2. Karen (a. decided not to use her phone for a couple of days b. enjoyed texting friends on the weekend c. took her phone to bed with her).

3. Karen (a. did well on her test b. didn't study much for her test c. is ready for her test).

M: Hey, Karen. I didn't ¹_____ from you on the weekend. Is everything OK?

W: Hi, Zack. Yeah, everything's fine—I just put my smartphone to bed for a ²_____ of days.

M: What do you ³_____?

W: Well, I was studying for a big test on Friday night, but I kept getting ⁴_____ notifications. I ended up ⁵_____ friends most of the night.

M: It's hard to study that ⁶_____, isn't it?

W: Right. So I decided to turn off my phone and put it in my desk ⁷_____.

M: It must have ⁸_____ great to study without being disturbed.

W: It *did*! I was much more ⁹_____. And I'm really well prepared for my test. ¹⁰_____, my phone is still in the drawer. Ha ha ha!

Notes put ... to bed …を考えないようにする　notification 通知　end up 結局…する　disturb 邪魔をする

Tips for Listening　　　暗い L の発音に注意して聞こう

L /l/ の音は、①語中で《母音 + /l/ +子音》の並びになった時（例 milk）、②語末にくる時（例 pencil）にこもった「オ」のように発音されます。これを「暗い L (dark L)」と呼びます。

Task 音声を聞いて空欄に入る語句を書きましょう。その後、音声を聞いてリピートしましょう。　🎧 03

1. I don't know that _____ _____.

2. I _____ _____ and sick now.

3. There were a lot of _____ who needed _____.

Grammar Preview　動名詞

動詞を -ing 形にすることによって「…すること」という意味を表したものを動名詞と呼びます。動名詞は名詞としての役割を果たすため、文の主語や目的語、補語、前置詞の目的語として使うことができます。

例 **Eating** too much is not good for your health. （食べすぎは健康に良くありません）

Meg likes **drawing** pictures. （メグは絵を描くことが好きです）

I'm interested in **learning** about Thai culture. （私はタイ文化を学ぶことに興味があります）

Task 日本語に合うように、空欄に適切な語句を入れましょう。

1. 寝る前にスマートフォンを使うのは避ける（avoid）べきです。

   You should _____ before you go to sleep.

2. 彼は人を笑わせる（laugh）ことが得意です。

   He _____.

3. 熱いお風呂に入ることはストレスを和らげます。

   _____ can relieve your stress.

Vocabulary Preview

語群の中から適切な語句を選び、**1.** ~ **6.** の空欄に入れましょう。

concentration （集中力）	beneficial （有益な）	refrain （…を控える）
overload （過剰な状態）	partial （部分的な）	strain （…を痛める）

1. Please _____ from eating or drinking inside the building.

2. You'll _____ your back if you try to lift that box by yourself.

3. In some restaurants and cafés, we are faced with an _____ of choices.

4. Regular exercise is _____ to one's health.

5. Chess and shogi are games that require great _____.

6. Due to the poor weather, the event was only a _____ success.

デジタル・デトックスに関する **Short Talk** を聞き、次の A ～ C に取り組みましょう。

Note detox 解毒、デトックス（detoxification の短縮形）

A **Short Talk** を聞き、内容に合うものを a. ～ c. の中から１つずつ選びましょう。 04

1. What problem related to the overuse of digital devices is not mentioned?

   a. Lack of sleep

   b. Neck and shoulder pain

   c. Eye damage

2. What is one benefit of a digital detox that is mentioned?

   a. It saves people both time and money.

   b. It gives people the opportunity to do other things.

   c. It allows people to try new types of digital devices.

B 空欄に適切な語 (句) を入れて **Short Talk** の内容をまとめましょう。

Recap

What is digital detox?

➡ A period of time when a person [1]_____ from using digital devices

What are some effects of overusing digital devices?

➡ reducing one's quality of sleep, causing eye [2]_____ and vision problems, resulting in serious [3]_____, making people unable to complete simple [4]_____

What are some benefits of a digital detox?

➡ It ① leads to better sleep, more energy, improved [5]_____ and less stress, ② makes people more [6]_____ of what's happening around them, ③ allows people to spend more time with family and friends, enjoy [7]_____ or try new things.

➡ Even a [8]_____ detox can be good for one's general health and happiness.

C 以下を参考にしながら、**Short Talk** の内容のリテリングをしましょう。

Retell

※空欄に記入する必要はありません

Digital detox refers to a period of time when [1]▓▓▓▓▓▓▓. The overuse of these technologies can [2]▓▓▓▓▓▓▓. Some people may become unable to complete simple tasks.

A digital detox can be beneficial in a number of ways. First, it leads to [3]▓▓▓▓▓▓▓. Second, it makes people [4]▓▓▓▓▓▓▓. Finally, it allows people to [5]▓▓▓▓▓▓▓. Even a partial detox, such as [6]▓▓▓▓▓▓▓, can be good for one's general health and happiness.

頻度とは、ある行為や状態がどの程度の期間や間隔を置いて起きるのかを意味します。英語には以下のような頻度を表す表現があります。

☐ **always**（いつも）、**usually**（普段、たいてい）、**often**（よく、しばしば）、**sometimes**（時々）、**occasionally**（たまに）、**rarely / seldom / hardly ever**（めったに…ない）、**never**（決して…ない）

例 I **usually** watch YouTube videos before I go to bed.
(私は普段寝る前に YouTube 動画を観ます)

例 Professor Tanaka **seldom** takes attendance in his class.
(田中教授は授業でめったに出席を取りません)

例 She is **never** late for work.（彼女は決して仕事に遅刻しません）

☐ **X times a day [week, month, year]**（1 日［週間・カ月・年］に X 回）

※ 1 回、2 回の場合はそれぞれ once a day、twice a week のように言います。

例 I work part-time **three times a week.**（私は週 3 回アルバイトをします）

☐ 「時々」の言い換え **from time to time / now and then**

例 I visit my grandparents **from time to time.**（私は時々祖父母を訪ねます）

Speak Out

次の **A** と **B** に取り組み、デジタル機器との関わり方についての会話をしましょう。

A 学習した表現を使って、次の会話文を完成させましょう。完成後、ペアで練習しましょう。
_____ には、**Tips for Speaking** の表現が入ります。

A: How often do you use your smartphone?

B: I _____ use it—probably about _____ a day. How about you?

A: I use mine about _____. What do you mainly use your phone for?

B: Many things—_____, _____, _____
and so on. And you?

A: _____
_____.

B 次の質問についてパートナーと会話をしましょう。必要に応じて、**Useful Vocabulary and Expressions** の表現を使ってみましょう。

1. Do you think you spend too much time using your smartphone or social media sites? Would you ever consider a digital detox like the one described in the short talk?

> Me

> My Partner

2. What are your favorite social media platforms (Facebook, Twitter, Instagram, YouTube, etc.) or internet sites? Why do you like them?

> Me

> My Partner

Useful Vocabulary and Expressions

- tablet (device) (タブレット端末)
- disconnect from ... (…を断つ)
- physical [mental] health (身体の [心の] 健康)
- digital habit (電子機器を使う習慣)
- get addicted to social media (ソーシャルメディアに依存する)
- refrain from using one's smartphone (スマートフォンを使わないようにする)
- use one's smartphone while walking (歩きスマホをする)
- kill time surfing the internet (インターネットを閲覧して時間をつぶす)
- social media platform (SNS のサイト)
- productive (生産的な)
- app (アプリ)
- take a break (休憩を取る)

17

Unit 2 The Sharing Economy

Talk with Your Partner

次の質問についてペアで会話をしましょう。

Q1 What are some things you have borrowed from or lent to other people?

A _____

Q2 Why do you think do-it yourself (DIY) is popular these days?

A _____

Listen to the Dialogue

Luke と友人の会話を聞き、次の A ～ C に取り組みましょう。

A 会話を聞き、イラストの内容が話の順番になるよう、1 ～ 4 の番号を記入しましょう。 05

B 会話の内容について、最も適切な語 (句) の記号を a. ～ c. の中から 1 つずつ選びましょう。

1. The farmer and his wife (a. gave   b. are lending   c. are renting) their car to Luke.

2. Luke teaches Jacob on (a. weekends   b. Tuesday nights   c. Thursday evenings).

3. On the farm, Luke (a. eats for free   b. cooks meals for the family   c. earns extra money as a tutor).

C　もう一度会話を聞き、空欄に入る語を記入しましょう。 05

W: I heard you were looking for a summer job, Luke. Have you ¹_____ one yet?

M: Yes, I'm working on a farm just ²_____ the city.

W: That sounds like fun. But ³_____ do you get there? You don't have a car, do you?

M: No, but the ⁴_____ and his wife are letting me use theirs. They mostly use their truck to get ⁵_____.

W: Oh, that's very nice of them, isn't it?

M: Yeah! So, to return the favor, I buy their groceries for them. I also tutor their son Jacob in ⁶_____ for a few hours on Thursday evenings. He's a ⁷_____ high school student.

W: Do they pay you ⁸_____ for that?

M: They ⁹_____, but I said no. I think the money they're paying me to work on their farm is already enough—and I get free ¹⁰_____!

Notes return the favor お返しに groceries 食料 tutor 個人教授をする

Tips for Listening　　/s/ と /ʃ/ の違いに注意して聞こう

sea (/s/) と she (/ʃ/) の出だしの子音は、カタカナにすると「シ」になりますが、異なる音です。/s/は日本語のサ・ス・セ・ソの出だしの音、/ʃ/ は日本語のシの出だしの音をイメージすると良いでしょう。両者を混同すると、正確な意味を伝えたり聞き取ったりすることができなくなるので注意が必要です。

Task 音声を聞いて空欄に単語を書きましょう。その後、音声を聞いてリピートしましょう。 06

1. _____　　　2. _____

3. _____　　　4. _____

5. _____　　　6. _____

7. _____　　　8. _____

Grammar Preview | 現在分詞の形容詞的用法

現在分詞（動詞の -ing 形）には、「…している」という意味を名詞に付け加える用法があります。

例 Nowadays, there are few people **reading** newspapers on trains.

（最近では、電車で新聞を読んでいる人はほとんどいません）

We interviewed 100 students **majoring** in economics.

（私たちは経済学を専攻している 100 人の学生にインタビューをしました）。

Task 日本語に合うように、空欄に適切な語句を入れましょう。

1. 電話で話している人はスミスさんです。

    The man _____ is Mr. Smith.

2. これは、実験結果を示しているグラフです。

    This is a graph _____.

3. キウィはニュージーランド（New Zealand）にしか生息していない鳥です。

    The kiwi is a bird _____.

Vocabulary Preview

語群の中から適切な語句を選び、**1. ～ 6.** の空欄に入れましょう。

> fee （費用）   rely （…を頼る）   virtue （美徳）
>
> spare （余分の）   alternative （代わりになる物）   underutilized （活用されていない）

1. Helen's greatest _____ is her honesty.

2. Paul is a fine worker, but his skills are _____ by his company.

3. The entrance _____ for the museum is $15.

4. Tofu is a great _____ to meat.

5. He spends most of his _____ time reading history books.

6. Many university students _____ on their parents for financial support.

共有経済に関する **Short Talk** を聞き、次の A ～ C に取り組みましょう。

A **Short Talk** を聞き、内容に合うものを a. ～ c. の中から１つずつ選びましょう。 07

1. What is the sharing economy based on?

   a. People using each other's property and resources
   b. Individuals buying and selling stocks
   b. Countries sharing goods and services

2. In a sharing economy, how might a do-it-yourselfer earn extra money?

   a. By starting his own company
   b. By renting some of his tools
   c. By working part-time for a building company

B　空欄に適切な語 (句) を入れて **Short Talk** の内容をまとめましょう。

Recap

- Sharing as a virtue. ➡ It builds friendships, ¹_____ and trust.
- the sharing economy
  - ➡ based on the idea of individuals sharing ²_____ goods and services with other individuals, usually for a ³_____
  - ➡ The internet conveniently ⁴_____ individual buyers and sellers, offering an ⁵_____ to purchasing goods and services offered by companies.
- Examples:
  - (1) A homeowner with a ⁶_____ bedroom earns a few extra dollars by offering the room to travelers looking for a place to stay the night.
  - (2) A DIY guy with a workshop full of power equipment connects with people in his area who want to use some ⁷_____ for a few hours.
- In a sharing economy, people ⁸_____ on each other for their needs, rather than on full-time businesses.

C　以下を参考にしながら、**Short Talk** の内容のリテリングをしましょう。

Retell ※空欄に記入する必要はありません

From an early age, we are taught that sharing is a virtue as it builds ¹_____. Recently, however, a new type of sharing called the sharing economy is happening. It's based on the idea of ²_____, usually for a fee. The internet conveniently connects ³_____, offering an alternative to ⁴_____ offered by companies. For example, a homeowner with a spare bedroom earns a few extra dollars by offering ⁵_____. Or a DIY guy with a workshop full of power equipment connects with people in his area who ⁶_____. In a sharing economy, people ⁷_____, rather than on full-time businesses.

《副詞 + speaking,》の副詞の部分に様々な語を入れることによって、これから話す内容に対して自分がどのようなスタンスを取るのかを明確にすることができます。

☐ **frankly speaking**（率直に言うと）

例 Frankly speaking, we are short of staff. （率直に言うと、人手不足です）

※ in all honesty や to tell the truth を使うこともできる。

☐ **actually**（実は）

例 Actually, I want to be an actor rather than work at a company.

（実は、会社勤めをするのではなく、俳優になりたいです）

☐ **roughly speaking**（大雑把に言うと）

例 Roughly speaking, a *yurukyara* is a kind of mascot.

（大雑把に言うと、ゆるキャラとはマスコットの一種です）

☐ **generally speaking**（一般的に言うと）

例 Generally speaking, tall players have an advantage in basketball.

（一般的に言うと、バスケットボールでは背の高い選手の方が有利です）※ in general を使うこともできる。

Speak Out

次の **A** と **B** に取り組み、共有経済や働き方について会話をしましょう。

A 学習した表現を使って、次の会話文を完成させましょう。完成後、ペアで練習しましょう。
_____ には、**Tips for Speaking** の表現が入ります。

A: I saw you cutting Mr. and Mrs. Baker's grass the other day. Do they pay well?

B: _____, I do it for free. In exchange, Mr. and Mrs. Baker let me use their lawn mower to cut other people's grass in the neighborhood.

A: Hey, that's a great arrangement. _____?

B: Well, it depends on the size of the lawn, but, _____, I get $25.

A: That's _____. Professional services usually charge $50 or $60.

Notes in exchange 引き換えに lawn mower 芝刈り機 arrangement 取り決め

B 次の質問についてパートナーと会話をしましょう。必要に応じて、**Useful Vocabulary and Expressions** の表現を使ってみましょう。

1. Besides working for a company, what are some things you could do to earn some extra money?

Me

My Partner

2. Do you think a sharing economy is beneficial to society? Why or why not?

Me

My Partner

Useful Vocabulary and Expressions

- goods（モノ）
- skill（技能）
- expertise（専門的な技能）
- barter（物々交換をする）
- local workers（地域での働き手）
- match（マッチする）
- flea market（フリーマーケット）
- stay at a private home（民泊をする）
- make money through crowdfuding（クラウドファンディングで資金を集める）
- provide childcare support（子育て支援を提供する）
- use the housekeeping services（家事代行サービスを利用する）

Unit
3 Clothes & Fashion

Talk with Your Partner

次の質問についてペアで会話をしましょう。

Q1 What clothing items have you bought recently?

A _____

Q2 What do you usually wear to school?

A _____

26

Listen to the Dialogue

Tony と友人の古着についての会話を聞き、次の A ～ C に取り組みましょう。

A 会話を聞き、写真の内容が話の順番になるよう、1 ～ 4 の番号を記入しましょう。 08

a

b

c

d

B 会話の内容について、最も適切な語 (句) の記号を a. ～ c. の中から1つずつ選びましょう。

1. Tony bought his jeans (a. at a used clothing store   b. from an online site
   c. at a flea market*).   *flea market フリーマーケット

2. According to Tony, vintage clothes are (a. very good quality   b. hard to
   find   c. all expensive).

3. Fast fashion is (a. expensive   b. eco-friendly*   c. not made to
   last*).   *eco-friendly 環境にやさしい   last 長持ちする

27

C もう一度会話を聞き、空欄に入る語を記入しましょう。

W: I love your vintage clothes, Tony. Where did you get them?

M: I got this shirt at a ¹_____ clothing store. And I bought these jeans
   ²_____.

W: They must have ³_____ very expensive.

M: They were a little expensive, but not all vintage clothes are. I found this belt at
   a flea market for only ⁴_____. And these boots were my father's. You
   have to ⁵_____, too, that vintage clothes are high ⁶_____
   and last a long time.

W: Good ⁷_____. Fast fashion is inexpensive, but it isn't designed to be
   ⁸_____ for very long. It isn't very eco-friendly, is it?

M: No, not really. ... Hey, I'm going to a flea market on Sunday. If you're
   ⁹_____, why don't you come along?

W: I'd like that. Maybe I can find some vintage clothes for ¹⁰_____.

Tips for Listening 　二重母音に注意して聞こう

英語には、time の /aɪ/ のように 2 つの母音が連続する音があります。これを二重母音（dipthong）と呼びます。主な二重母音として、mouth の /aʊ/ や later の /eɪ/、only の /oʊ/、ride の /aɪ/、oil の /ɔɪ/ があります。二重母音の主役は最初の母音なので、2 つ目の母音はそれに軽く添えるような気持ちで発音されます。

Task 音声を聞いて、二重母音に注意して単語を空欄に書きましょう。その後、音声を聞いてリピートしましょう。

09

1. _____   2. _____
3. _____   4. _____
5. _____   6. _____
7. _____   8. _____

Grammar Preview　可算名詞と不可算名詞

名詞は、数えられる名詞（可算名詞）と数えられない名詞（不可算名詞）に分けることができます。例えば、前者には book や computer、day といった語が含まれ、後者には money や water などの物質名詞や、furniture や baggage などの集合名詞、happiness や education などの抽象名詞が含まれます。可算名詞は複数形になるのに対して、不可算名詞は通例、複数形にはなりません。ただし、time（回数は可算、時間は不可算）のように、同じ名詞でも可算名詞・不可算名詞いずれとしても用いられるものがあります。

Task 名詞の形に注目して、次の日本語を英語にしましょう。

1. このハンカチは綿 100% です。

   _____

2. 彼はネクタイを 50 本以上持っています。

   _____

3. すみません、男性用の靴はどこにありますか。

   _____

Vocabulary Preview

語群の中から適切な語句を選び、1. ～ 6. の空欄に入れましょう。

> practical（実用的な）　　affordable（手頃な）
> jersey（ジャージー［毛・綿・絹・化繊などの糸を用いて編んだ生地］）
> influential（影響力のある）　reflect（反映する）　popularize（普及する）

1. He works for a very large and _____ newspaper.

2. Her books _____ her thoughts and ideas.

3. Smartphones have really helped to _____ mobile apps.

4. _____ is commonly used to make shirts, dresses, pajamas and more.

5. Small cars are _____ for city driving.

6. The shop sells high quality goods at _____ prices.

ココ・シャネルに関する **Short Talk** を聞き、次の A ～ C に取り組みましょう。

A **Short Talk** を聞き、内容に合うものを **a.** ～ **c.** の中から1つずつ選びましょう。 10

1. What did Chanel hope to achieve through her designs?

   a. Freedom of movement

   b. Unique color combinations

   c. Clothes that could be worn anywhere

2. What is Chanel known for?

   a. Inventing women's pants

   b. Making comfortable underwear for men

   c. Being the first woman to use jersey for her designs

B 空欄に適切な語 (句) を入れて **Short Talk** の内容をまとめましょう。

Recap

Coco Chanel was the most influential fashion ¹_____ of the 20th century, and wanted women to be able to move and breathe in their clothes.

● In the early 1920's, women were still expected to wear ²_____ clothing like corsets and tight dresses for certain leisure activities.

  (1) She found this ³_____, so one day she wore pants while horseback riding.

  (2) She wore wide-leg pants instead of a ⁴_____ while on vacation in France.

   ➡ Women began to ⁵_____ her example.

   ➡ She didn't invent women's pants, but she ⁶_____ them.

● She used jersey for women's wear, which was unusual because it had mostly been used for men's ⁷_____.

   ➡ She created jersey ⁸_____ that were not only elegant, but also comfortable, practical and affordable—and women loved them.

C 以下を参考にしながら、**Short Talk** の内容のリテリングをしましょう。

Retell ※空欄に記入する必要はありません

Coco Chanel was perhaps the most influential fashion designer of the 20th century. She once said, "¹_____," and her designs reflected those words. She wanted women to ²_____, just like men did in theirs.

In the early 1920's, women were still expected to wear ³_____ for certain leisure activities. Chanel found this strange, so one day she ⁴_____. Later, she wore ⁵_____. Although Chanel didn't invent women's pants, she ⁶_____.

Chanel was the first woman to use jersey for women's wear. It was an unusual choice because it ⁷_____. She created jersey garments that were ⁸_____—and women loved them.

会話では、途中で話題を変えたり、脱線から話題を戻したりする場面が多くあります。英語では以下のような定型表現があります。

☐ **話題を変える**

By the way （ところで）

To change the subject （話題を変えますが）　※ Changing the subject と言うこともできる。

Speaking of ... （…と言えば）

That reminds me. （それで思い出しましたが）　※相手の発言に関連することを思いついた時に使う。

This is off topic, but ... （話は変わりますが、…）

☐ **話題を戻す**

Let's get back to the main point. （話を元に戻しましょう）

※ Going back to the main point と言うこともできる。

Let's get back on track. （話を元に戻しましょう）

※話題がそれている時は、We are getting off track. と言う。

Seriously though, ... （いや、真面目な話）　※真面目な話に戻す時に使う。

Speak Out

次の **A** と **B** に取り組み、衣類やファッションについての会話をしましょう。

A 学習した表現を使って、次の会話文を完成させましょう。完成後、ペアで練習しましょう。＿＿＿＿には、**Tips for Speaking** の表現が入ります。

A: Do you know where Cathy is? I need to talk to her about something.

B: She went shopping with Emily, I think. Oh, ＿＿＿＿＿＿＿＿＿, did you go to that vintage clothing store I told you about?

A: What? ... No, not yet. ＿＿＿＿＿＿＿＿ Do you have Cathy's smartphone number? It's really important that I talk to her right away.

B: Oh, sorry. I didn't know it was important. ＿＿＿＿＿＿＿＿＿＿＿.

B 次の質問についてパートナーと会話をしましょう。必要に応じて、**Useful Vocabulary and Expressions** の表現を使ってみましょう。

1. What do you do with your old clothing? Throw it away? Sell it? Give it away?

> Me

> My Partner

2. Where do you like to buy your clothes? Why do you like that store?

> Me

> My Partner

Useful Vocabulary and Expressions

- casual clothes (私服)
- fashionable (おしゃれな)
- loose (ゆったりした)
- gaudy (派手な)
- hoodie (パーカー)
- lightweight clothes (薄着)
- shorts (短パン)
- one-size-fits-all (フリーサイズ)
- sweatshirt (トレーナー)
- long-sleeved [short-sleeved] shirt (長袖 [半袖] シャツ)
- get dressed (身支度をする)
- put on [take off] a T-shirt (T シャツを着る [脱ぐ])
- tuck in one's shirt (シャツをズボンに入れる)
- turn [roll] up one's sleeves (袖をまくる)

33

Talk with Your Partner

次の質問についてペアで会話をしましょう。

Q1 Which do you prefer, dogs or cats? Why?

A _____

Q2 Can you name four animals that are known for their intelligence?

A _____

Listen to the Dialogue

カラスの知能についての会話を聞き、次の A ～ C に取り組みましょう。

A 会話を聞き、イラストの内容が話の順番になるよう、1 ～ 4 の番号を記入しましょう。

B 会話の内容について、最も適切な語 (句) の記号を a. ～ c. の中から1つずつ選びましょう。

1. The man thinks the crow* is (a. beautiful   b. big   c. noisy).   *crow カラス

2. Crows (a. have a good memory   b. have a small brain for their body size
    c. often attack people for no reason).

3. According to the conversation, crows (a. do not like walnuts   b. are good
    at getting food   c. drink very little water).

C もう一度会話を聞き、空欄に入る語を記入しましょう。

W: This park is really beautiful, isn't it?

M: Yeah, it's great ... ¹_____ for the crow in that tree over there. It's really noisy. I'm going to ²_____ it away.

W: No, don't do that. And don't look at it! Crows ³_____ faces and will ⁴_____ people if they feel threatened.

M: That's good to know. Thank you.

W: Yeah, crows have an excellent ⁵_____, and they're very intelligent. They can catch food from ⁶_____ in the ground and trees with a small stick.

M: Ah, now that you mention it, I once read a story where crows ⁷_____ in a city in Japan ⁸_____ walnuts onto the roads. Cars would then drive over the nuts and ⁹_____ them open.

W: ... And the crows would then eat the small ¹⁰_____. How clever!

Notes threatened 脅威にさらされた now that you mention it 言われてみれば How clever! 何て賢いの！

| Tips for Listening | 前置詞 to の弱形に注意して聞こう |

前置詞 to には、強く読まれる発音（強形）と弱く読まれる発音（弱形）があります。前者は /túː/、後者は /tə/ と発音されます。to を強調する必要がない限り、会話では /tə/ と発音するのが一般的です。

Task 音声を聞いて空欄に入る語句を書きましょう。その後、音声を聞いてリピートしましょう。　🎧 12

1. I _____ _____ turn in my essay by tomorrow.

2. My father has already _____ _____ the office.

3. Do you have _____ _____ do?

4. Would you _____ _____ order a drink?

5. _____ _____ the right at the next corner.

6. It's _____ _____ go.

Grammar Preview　直前の名詞の内容を説明する to 不定詞（形容詞的用法）

to 不定詞には、前に来る名詞の内容を説明する働きがあります。この名詞と to 不定詞の関係は、《同格》
と呼ばれます。

例 In Japan, women won <u>the right</u> **to vote** in 1925.
　　（日本では，1925 年に女性が参政権を得ました）

Dogs have <u>the ability</u> **to read** human emotions.（イヌには人間の感情を読む能力があります）

He has <u>a desire</u> **to be** a politician.（彼には政治家になるという願望があります）

Task 日本語に合うように、空欄に適切な語句を入れましょう。

1.　父は私たちを北海道に連れていくと約束しました。

　　My father made a ＿＿＿＿＿＿＿＿＿＿＿＿＿＿＿＿＿＿＿＿＿＿＿＿＿＿＿＿ .

2.　彼は留学をするという決断をしました。

　　He made a ＿＿＿＿＿＿＿＿＿＿＿＿＿＿＿＿＿＿＿＿＿＿＿＿＿＿＿＿＿＿ .

3.　怒った時、彼女には歩くのが速くなる傾向（tendency）があります。

　　She has a ＿＿＿＿＿＿＿＿＿＿＿＿＿＿＿＿＿＿＿＿＿＿＿ when she gets angry.

Vocabulary　Preview

語群の中から適切な語句を選び、**1. ～ 6.** の空欄に入れましょう。

> characteristic（特徴）　capability（能力）　process（処理する）
> recognize（認識する）　species（種）　adapt（適応する）

1.　I didn't ＿＿＿＿＿＿＿ my friend because I hadn't seen him in more than
　　20 years.

2.　It takes time for people to ＿＿＿＿＿＿＿ to a new culture.

3.　There about one million ＿＿＿＿＿＿＿ of insects.

4.　Mike's honesty is his best ＿＿＿＿＿＿＿ .

5.　The human brain is able to ＿＿＿＿＿＿＿ information very quickly.

6.　Zoo animals often lose the ＿＿＿＿＿＿＿ of catching food for themselves.

動物の知能に関する **Short Talk** を聞き、次の **A** ～ **C** に取り組みましょう。

A **Short Talk** を聞き、内容に合うものを **a.** ～ **c.** の中から１つずつ選びましょう。 13

1. What is one way a person's intelligence is measured?

   a. By the size of their brain
   b. By their communication ability
   c. By their ability to find food

2. How do animals adapt to their surroundings?

   a. They form social groups.
   b. They communicate with other animals.
   c. They learn new skills.

B 空欄に適切な語 (句) を入れて **Short Talk** の内容をまとめましょう。

Recap

- Measuring human intelligence
  - the ability to [1]understand and use spoken and written language, [2]1_____ things, [3]recognize faces and scenes, [4]notice small [2]_____, and [5]solve [3]_____ problems
- Measuring animal intelligence
  - the way animals learn [4]_____ that enable them to live and to adapt to their environments
- Examples of animal intelligence
  - the ability to adapt to their [5]_____ by learning to change their habits and [6]_____
  - the ability to [7]_____ social groups (ex. elephants and dolphins)
    - → All of these abilities are made possible by their ability to [8]_____ information.

C 以下を参考にしながら、 **Short Talk** の内容のリテリングをしましょう。

Retell   ※空欄に記入する必要はありません

Human intelligence may be measured in various ways such as the ability to understand and use [1]_____, the ability to visualize things, recognize faces and scenes, or notice small details, and the ability to solve mathematical problems. Animal intelligence is measured by [2]_____ that enable them to live and to adapt to their environments.

Animals are able to adapt to their surroundings by [3]_____. Many animals are also capable of [4]_____. All of these characteristics are made possible by [5]_____. By studying this ability, we can better understand [6]_____.

会話等で例を挙げる際、英語では以下のような表現を使うことができます。

☐ **for example / for instance**

例 Japan has many famous entrepreneurs. **For example**, Ando Momofuku is known as the inventor of instant noodles.

(日本には多くの有名な起業家がいます。例えば、安藤百福は、インスタント麺の発明者として知られています)

☐ **like ...**

例 I love fruits **like** blueberries, mangos and pineapples.

(私はブルーベリーやマンゴー、パイナップルといった果物が大好きです)

☐ **such as ...**

例 *Natto* is full of nutrients **such as** Vitamin K, protein and fiber.

(納豆には、ビタミンKやタンパク質、食物繊維といった栄養素が豊富に含まれています)

☐ **To give an example, ... / Let me give you an example. ...**

例 Tom is a very generous person. **To give an example**, he gave me his old car. (トムはとても気前の良い人です。例えば、彼は私に前に使っていた車をくれました)

Speak Out

次の **A** と **B** に取り組み、動物や動物の知能についての会話をしましょう。

A 学習した表現を使って、次の会話文を完成させましょう。完成後、ペアで練習しましょう。
_____ には、**Tips for Speaking** の表現が入ります。

A: What do you think the most intelligent animal is?

B: I have no idea, but _____ are quite smart, I think.

A: And why do you say that?

B: Well, _____, they can _____ and _____.

How about you? What animal do you think is the smartest?

A: I don't know, either, but I'll say _____. They _____

_____.

40

B 次の質問についてパートナーと会話をしましょう。必要に応じて、**Useful Vocabulary and Expressions** の表現を使ってみましょう。

1. Some animals are superior* to humans in certain ways. Give a few examples.
   *…より優れている

Me

My Partner

2. If you could be any animal, what would you be? Why?

Me

My Partner

Useful Vocabulary and Expressions

- evolution (進化)
- adaptable (適応力のある)
- sociable (社交性のある)
- instinctively (本能的に)
- survival of the fittest (適者生存)
- predator (捕食者)
- tool (道具)
- smart (頭が良い)
- mammal (哺乳類)
- mimic (真似する)
- symbol (記号)
- brain (脳)
- carry out complex tasks (複雑な作業を行う)
- have a good memory (記憶力が優れている)
- understand and display emotions (感情を理解し、表現する)
- conduct animal experiments (動物実験を行う)

Unit 5 The Power of Grit

Talk with Your Partner

次の質問についてペアで会話をしましょう。

Q1 What are two goals that you hope to achieve in the next few years?

A _____

Q2 What are two of your long-term goals?

A _____

Listen to the Dialogue

偉大なプロバスケットボールの選手であったマイケル・ジョーダンの高校時代のエピソードについての会話を聞き、次の A 〜 C に取り組みましょう。

A 会話を聞き、イラストの内容が話の順番になるよう、1 〜 4 の番号を記入しましょう。

B 会話の内容について、最も適切な語 (句) の記号を a. 〜 c. の中から1つずつ選びましょう。

1. Michael Jordan was cut* from his (a. junior high school　b. high school
   c. college) basketball team.　*was cut 退部させられた

2. After getting cut, Jordan (a. gave up his dream　b. started to dream
   c. continued to follow his dream) of becoming a professional player.

3. To stay motivated, Jordan imagined himself (a. playing professionally
   b. talking with his teammates in the locker room　c. looking at a list).

C もう一度会話を聞き、空欄に入る語を記入しましょう。 14

W: Are you going to try out for the basketball team ¹_____ this year, Stan?

M: No, I'm not good ²_____. Everyone is better than me.

W: You know, Michael Jordan was cut from his high school basketball team for not ³_____ good enough.

M: Michael Jordan? Really?

W: It's true. After he got cut, he went home and ⁴_____ in his room. But he never gave up his ⁵_____ of becoming a professional basketball player.

M: How did he ⁶_____ motivated?

W: Whenever he got ⁷_____ while practicing and thought about stopping, he would close his eyes and see the ⁸_____ in the locker room without his name on it. That motivated him to keep going and practice even ⁹_____.

M: And he went on to become one of the ¹⁰_____ players ever! ... Maybe I'll try out for the team after all. I better start practicing.

Notes try out 入団テストを受ける　after all 結局

Tips for Listening ⟩ リエゾン（連結）に注意して聞こう

英語では、《子音＋母音》が連続する時に両者がつながって発音されます。これをリエゾン（連結）と呼びます。単語を個々に発音する場合と異なった音に聞こえるので注意しましょう。

Task 音声を聞いて空欄に入る語句を書きましょう。その後、音声を聞いてリピートしましょう。 15

1. I'll be _____ _____ _____ few minutes.

2. Why don't you _____ _____ _____ try?

3. Do you _____ _____ _____?

Grammar Preview　《目的》を表す to 不定詞

to 不定詞には、「…するために」という《目的》を表す用法があります。《目的》の意味合いを明確にしたい場合は、in order [so as] to 不定詞を使うことも可能です。

例 I have to get up early tomorrow **to catch** the first train.

（始発電車に乗るために、私は明日早起きをしなければなりません）

In order to pass the test, you must study much harder.

（試験に合格するためには、もっと一生懸命勉強しなければなりません）

Task 日本語に合うように、空欄に適切な語句を入れましょう。

1. 昨日私は友人たちを見送る（see ... off）ために空港に行きました。

   Yesterday, I went to the airport _____.

2. 彼女はニューヨークに行くためにお金を貯めています。

   She is saving money _____.

3. あなたの質問に答えるためには、我々はもっと研究をする必要があります。

   _____, we need to do more research.

Vocabulary Preview

語群の中から適切な語句を選び、1. ～ 6. の空欄に入れましょう。

emerge （現れる）	perseverance （忍耐）	underachieve （能力以下の成績をおさめる）
passion （情熱）	predictor （予測するもの）	psychologist （心理学者）

1. There are many reasons why people _____.

2. Tom is a sports _____, working with athletes in various sports.

3. Information about the accident is just beginning to _____.

4. The best _____ of future behavior is past behavior.

5. She sings with great _____ every time she performs on stage.

6. _____ is failing nine times and succeeding on the tenth try.

アンジェラ・ダックワース氏に関する **Short Talk** を聞き、次の A ～ C に取り組みましょう。

A **Short Talk** を聞き、内容に合うものを a. ～ c. の中から1つずつ選びましょう。 16

1. Why did Duckworth leave her job as a teacher?

   a. She wanted to learn more about how people achieve success.

   b. She no longer enjoyed it.

   c. She wanted to become a university professor.

2. What did Duckworth discover about "grit"?

   a. It is found in underachievers.

   b. It is a predictor of long-term success.

   c. It is only useful for achieving short-term-goals.

B 空欄に適切な語 (句) を入れて **Short Talk** の内容をまとめましょう。

Recap

At a school in New York

Angela noticed some students with the highest IQ scores were ¹_____ ,
while others with lower scores were among her top performers.

→ Does success in school and life depend on much more than simply one's
²_____ to learn quickly and easily?

As a psychologist

Angela studied children and adults in various ³_____ situations to
answer one question, "Who will be successful and why?"

Findings   One ⁴_____ that constantly emerged as a predictor of achievement

→ "grit" ＝ a combination of ⁵_____ and ⁶_____

- Although education, intelligence, family and money all play a role in
  achieving ⁷_____ success, she believes that what ⁸_____ most is grit.

C 以下を参考にしながら、**Short Talk** の内容のリテリングをしましょう。

Retell   ※空欄に記入する必要はありません

At the age of 27, Angela Duckworth started ¹_____ in New York and
noticed that some students with the highest IQ scores ²_____ , while
others with lower scores were among her top performers.

As a psychologist, she studied children and adults in various challenging
situations to answer one question: ³_____ ? In her studies, she found
out that a predictor of achievement was ⁴_____ that she calls "grit."
Although ⁵_____ all play a role in achieving long-term success, she
believes that ⁶_____ .

会話では、相手の言っていることが聞こえなかったり、よく理解できなかったりする場面があります。その際、以下のような表現を使うことができます。

☐ **Pardon? / Sorry? / Excuse me?** （もう一度お願いします）

※ I beg your pardon? と言うと丁寧な表現になる。

☐ **Could [Can] you say that again?** （もう一度おっしゃってくれませんか）

※ Could の方が Can よりも丁寧な表現

☐ **What's that?** （何と言いましたか）

☐ **I'm sorry, but I couldn't hear what you said.**

（すみません、 おっしゃったことが聞き取れませんでした）

☐ **Sorry, I didn't catch that.** （すみません、 聞き逃しました）

☐ **Could you (kindly) repeat that?** （もう一度おっしゃっていただいてよろしいですか）

☐ **Would you mind saying that again?** （もう一度おっしゃっていただいてよろしいですか）

Speak Out

次の **A** と **B** に取り組み、成功するために必要なことについて会話をしましょう。

A 学習した表現を使って、次の会話文を完成させましょう。完成後、ペアで練習しましょう。
_____ には、**Tips for Speaking** の表現が入ります。

A: You had a basketball game against Central University last night. Did you win?

B: No, we got creamed again.

A: Sorry, but I _____. Could you _____?

B: We _____ ... we lost really badly. The score was 125 to 58.

A: That's too bad. What does the team need to do to get out of its slump?

B: We all need to _____, _____ and _____.

48

B 次の質問についてパートナーと会話をしましょう。必要に応じて、**Useful Vocabulary and Expressions** の表現を使ってみましょう。

1. Why do you think some people are more successful than others?

> **Me**

> **My Partner**

2. Do you agree with Professor Duckworth that "grit" (passion and perseverance) is a predictor of long-term success? Why or why not?

> **Me**

> **My Partner**

Useful Vocabulary and Expressions

- motivation（モチベーション）
- career（進路、キャリア）
- a strong will（強い意志）
- praise（褒める）
- progress（進捗状況）
- advice（アドバイス）
- long-term [short-term] goal（長期［短期］目標）
- achieve（達成する）
- encourage（…を励ます）
- plan（計画［する]）
- failure（失敗）
- look back（振り返る）
- objectively（客観的に）
- keep a record of …（…の記録を取る）
- be stuck in a slump（スランプに陥る）/ break out of a slump（スランプを脱する）
- set clear goals（明確な目標を決める）
- make an effort / try hard（努力をする）
- pursue one's dream（夢を追い続ける）
- not give up（諦めない）

Unit

6 Telework

Talk with Your Partner

次の質問についてペアで会話をしましょう。

Q1 What is one positive point about telework?

A _____

Q2 What is one negative point about telework?

A _____

Listen to the Dialogue

Jake と友人の働き方についての会話を聞き、次の **A** ～ **C** に取り組みましょう。

A　会話を聞き、イラストの内容が話の順番になるよう、1～4の番号を記入しましょう。

B　会話の内容について、最も適切な語 (句) の記号を **a.** ～ **c.** の中から1つずつ選びましょう。

1. "Workation" means (**a.** working creation　**b.** working relaxation
    c. working vacation).

2. Jake's "workation" will last (**a.** two months　**b.** a week　**c.** a couple of
    weeks).

3. Jake does (**a.** much less work　**b.** much more work　**c.** a little less work)
    at the cabin in Vermont* than he does at his office in New York.

    * **Vermont** バーモント州（米国北東部にある州）

W: Jake, your [1]_____ lives in New York, doesn't he?

M: That's right. He works in a large office [2]_____ in Manhattan. But right now he's doing a "workation."

W: A "workation"?

M: A working vacation. He and his family are [3]_____ at a cabin in Vermont for a couple of months. He [4]_____ one of the rooms as his office.

W: And his company [5]_____ him to do that?

M: Yes, they [6]_____ by email. He also has regular [7]_____ meetings with his manager and co-workers. He says he gets a lot more work [8]_____ at the cabin than he does at his Manhattan office.

W: [9]_____ about the vacation part of "workation"?

M: On weekends he enjoys spending time at the [10]_____ with his family.

Tips for Listening 語尾に来る /p/ /t/ /k/ /b/ /d/ /g/ の発音に注意して聞こう

cup や put、bag のように、単語の最後が /p/ /t/ /k/ /b/ /d/ /g/ の音で終わる時、これらの音が発音されない（脱落する）ことが多く見られます。それぞれの音を出す構えは行いますが、音は出ません。

Task 音声を聞いて空欄に入る語句を書きましょう。その後、音声を聞いてリピートしましょう。 🎧 18

1. Where did you _____ that _____?

2. _____ does this _____ mean?

3. There was a _____ _____ between our opinions.

Grammar Preview 《動詞 + 目的語 + *to do*》の形をとる動詞

My parents won't **allow me to have** a part-time job.（両親は私がアルバイトをするのを許してくれません）における allow のように、動詞の中には後ろに《目的語 + **to do**》の形を取るものがあります。以下は代表的な動詞です。

cause（原因となる）　　　　encourage（勧める、励ます）　　　enable（可能にする）

force（無理やり…させる）　　allow / permit（許す）

Task 日本語に合うように、空欄に適切な語句を入れましょう。

1. 食べすぎによって彼は病気になりました。

   Eating too much _____.

2. 担任の先生が私に留学をしてみなさいと励ましてくれました。

   My homeroom teacher _____.

3. インターネットによって私たちは世界中の人々とコミュニケーションを取ることができます。

   The internet _____.

Vocabulary Preview

語群の中から適切な語句を選び、**1.** ～ **6.** の空欄に入れましょう。

operations（運行）　　productive（生産的な）　　coined（［新語などを］造り出した）

ensure（確かめる）　　remotely（遠隔で）　　emergencies（緊急事態）

1. An American disc jockey _____ the phrase rock 'n' roll in 1951.

2. Thanks to technology, students can access library materials _____.

3. Please _____ that the windows are closed before you leave the room.

4. Due to the typhoon, train _____ were stopped.

5. You should keep some cash at home for _____.

6. People are more _____ when they manage their time well.

テレワークに関する **Short Talk** を聞き、次の **A** ～ **C** に取り組みましょう。

A   **Short Talk** を聞き、内容に合うものを **a.** ～ **c.** の中から1つずつ選びましょう。 19

1. Who was Jack Nilles?

   a. An astronaut   b. An engineer   c. A scientist

2. What is an advantage of telework for many workers?

   a. They can earn more money.

   b. They can enjoy a more flexible schedule.

   c. They can work fewer hours.

B 空欄に適切な語 (句) を入れて **Short Talk** の内容をまとめましょう。

Recap

Telework

- work that is done away from a central location with the help of ICT
- The term was [1]_____ by NASA scientist Jack Nilles in 1972.
- All people need is an internet [2]_____.

● Advantages:

(1) allows workers to use their time [3]_____

(2) reduces business [4]_____ such as office space and equipment

(3) ensures that [5]_____ can continue during emergencies

● Disadvantages:

Employees can become less [6]_____ and less [7]_____ due to the lack of [8]_____ communication.

C 以下を参考にしながら、**Short Talk** の内容のリテリングをしましょう。

Retell

※空欄に記入する必要はありません

Telework, or telecommuting, is work that [1]_____ with the help of [2]_____. The term was first coined by NASA scientist Jack Nilles in 1972. Thanks to technology, people can work from [3]_____, and all they need is [4]_____.

Telework allows many workers to [5]_____ by [6]_____. For companies, it reduces [7]_____. It also ensures that [8]_____ during emergencies. On the other hand, employees can become [9]_____ due to [10]_____.

日本語では相手に共感を求める際、「…ですよね？」や「…でしょ？」といった表現を使います。英語では以下のような表現を使うことができます。

☐ **付加疑問文**

He is so cool, **isn't he**?（彼はかっこいいですよね）

You go to work by bus, **don't you**?（あなたはバス通勤ですよね）

You had a such great time at the party, **didn't you**?（パーティーで楽しんだようですね）

The movie was not impressive, **was it**?（その映画は感動的ではなかったですよね）

☐ **..., right?**

You are from Hokkaido, **right**?（あなたは北海道出身ですよね）

We were supposed to meet here at two, **right**?（私たちは２時にここで集合でしたよね）

☐ **..., don't you think?**

Our company should promote more teleworking, **don't you think**?
（私たちの会社はテレワークを推進すべきですよね）

We should hold a meeting as soon as possible, **don't you think**?
（できるだけ早く会議を開くべきですよね）

Speak Out

次の **A** と **B** に取り組み、テレワークについての会話をしましょう。

A 学習した表現を使って、次の会話文を完成させましょう。完成後、ペアで練習しましょう。
＿＿＿＿＿＿には、**Tips for Speaking** の表現が入ります。

A: I think telework is a great way to work, ＿＿＿＿＿＿＿＿＿＿＿?

B: I guess it's good if you have a long commute. But ＿＿＿＿＿＿＿＿＿＿＿
＿＿＿＿＿＿＿＿＿＿＿＿＿＿＿＿＿, ＿＿＿＿＿＿＿＿＿＿＿?

A: Yeah, that's a good point, but I still like the idea of telework. For one thing,
＿＿＿＿＿＿＿＿＿＿＿＿＿＿＿＿＿＿＿＿＿＿＿＿.

Also, I think ＿＿＿＿＿＿＿＿＿＿＿＿＿＿＿＿＿＿
＿＿＿＿＿＿＿＿＿＿＿＿＿＿＿＿＿＿＿＿＿＿＿＿.

56

B 次の質問についてパートナーと会話をしましょう。必要に応じて、**Useful Vocabulary and Expressions** の表現を使ってみましょう。

1. Do you think teleworking will become more and more popular in the future? Why or why not?

> **Me**

> **My Partner**

2. Would you like to have a "workation" someday? Why or why not?

> **Me**

> **My Partner**

Useful Vocabulary and Expressions

- online video system （オンラインビデオシステム）
- work-life balance （ワークライフバランス）
- electricity bill （電気代）
- productivity （生産性）
- use time effectively [flexibly] （時間を有効に［柔軟に］使う）
- balance work and housework （仕事と家事を両立する）
- sit in front of the computer all day （一日中パソコンの前に座る）
- hold [have] an online meeting （オンライン会議をする）

- commute （通勤する）
- packed train （満員電車）
- working from home （在宅勤務）
- working hours （勤務時間）

Unit 7 Smart Cities

Talk with Your Partner

次の質問についてペアで会話をしましょう。

Q1 Can you name three examples of technology that we use every day?

A _____

Q2 What is one good point and one bad point about living in a big city?

A _____

Listen to the Dialogue

スマートシティについての会話を聞き、次の **A** 〜 **C** に取り組みましょう。

A 会話を聞き、写真の内容が話の順番になるよう、1〜4の番号を記入しましょう。

B 会話の内容について、最も適切な語（句）の記号を **a.** 〜 **c.** の中から1つずつ選びましょう。

1. The conversation is mainly about (a. solar power   b. smart technology
    c. public safety).

2. The area has smart (a. locks   b. mirrors   b. parking).

3. Smart bins* tell city workers (a. when they're full   b. what's in them
    c. how much the trash weighs).   *bin ごみ箱

W: This area of Auckland has a lot of smart ¹_____, like this solar-powered smart bench. You can ²_____ your smartphone or electric bicycle here, too.

M: Cool! What ³_____ smart technology does the area have?

W: Well, for our ⁴_____, there are smart lights that can be dimmed or brightened remotely. Some have sensors that check the air ⁵_____ and other things. This area also has smart parking. Parking spaces have sensors that ⁶_____ real-time data to your smartphone.

M: So you don't have to keep ⁷_____ around to find a parking space.

W: That's right. And that smart bin over there has sensors that tell ⁸_____ workers when it's time to ⁹_____ the trash.

M: Great! It's exciting to think about what cities will look like in the ¹⁰_____.

Notes Auckland オークランド (ニュージーランドの都市)   dimmed 薄暗くする

Tips for Listening   語の強勢に注意して聞こう

英語の単語には、強勢が置かれる音節が1つあります。誤った位置に強勢が置かれると、正確に聞き取ったり、伝えたりすることができなくなることがあります。単語を覚える際は、必ずどの音節が強く読まれるかを確認しましょう。

Task 音声を聞いて、単語の強勢が置かれる音節に〇をつけましょう。その後、音声を聞いてリピートしましょう。 🎧 21

1. tech・nol・o・gy
2. ef・fi・cien・cy
3. am・bu・lance
4. ex・am・ple
5. dis・patch
6. en・vi・ron・men・tal

Grammar Preview 比較級

ある物と別のものを比べて「A は（B より）…」と言う時は、形容詞または副詞を比較級という形にします。比較級には、small-smaller のような《-er 型》と、important-more important のような《more ＋原級型》、good / well-better のような《不規則変化型》があります。

例 For me, English is **easier** than math. （私にとって英語は数学よりも易しいです）

Friendship is **more important** than money. （お金よりも友情の方が大切です）

He can play soccer **better** than I. （彼は私よりも上手にサッカーをします）

Task 日本語に合うように、空欄に適切な語句を入れましょう。

1. 日本はフィンランドよりも大きいです。

   Japan _____ Finland.

2. ハリウッド映画よりも日本の映画の方が面白いと思います。

   I think Japanese movies _____ Hollywood movies.

3. 私は春よりも夏の方が好きです。

   I like summer _____ spring.

Vocabulary Preview

語群の中から適切な語句を選び、1. ～ 6. の空欄に入れましょう。

> alert （知らせる）　resident （住民）　dispatch （…を派遣する）
> urban （都市の）　flow （流れ）　efficiency （効率の良さ）

1. Traffic is a problem is many _____ areas.

2. Thanks to Mary's _____, we were able to complete the work in a few hours.

3. Jack has been a _____ of this city all his life.

4. Massage may help to improve blood _____ to certain parts of the body.

5. The government will _____ a team of experts to the accident site.

6. A nurse call button allows patients to _____ a nurse of their need for help.

スマートシティに関する **Short Talk** を聞き、次の **A** 〜 **C** に取り組みましょう。

A **Short Talk** を聞き、内容に合うものを **a.** 〜 **c.** の中から１つずつ選びましょう。 22

1. According to the talk, what is one of the main purposes of smart cities?

   a. To prevent them from becoming too large

   b. To protect the privacy of citizens

   c. To improve the quality of life of residents

2. According to the passage, how can smart cities improve healthcare systems?

   a. By remotely monitoring patients

   b. By providing free medicine

   c. By increasing the number of doctors and support staff

B 空欄に適切な語（句）を入れて **Short Talk** の内容をまとめましょう。

Recap

- By 2050, nearly 70% of the world's population will live in [1]_____ areas.
  → increasing environmental, social and economic challenges
- Smart cities use technology [1] to improve [2]_____ and the quality of services, and [2] to make everyday life easier, more convenient and safer for [3]_____.
- Examples of how smart cities might look
  - controlling traffic lights and improving traffic flow → faster daily [4]_____
  - automated [5]_____ systems, where smart devices monitor patients at home
    → Doctors and [6]_____ could be dispatched based on the data received, or medications could be delivered by [7]_____.
  - Crime may be reduced by installing smart cameras and security systems that would [8]_____ police of possible crimes.

C 以下を参考にしながら、**Short Talk** の内容のリテリングをしましょう。

Retell   ※空欄に記入する必要はありません

By 2050, [1]_____ will live in urban areas. Increasing environmental, social and economic challenges can be overcome by making our cities "smarter." Smart cities use technology to [2]_____, and to [3]_____.

Smart cities could make our daily commute faster by [4]_____. Cities can have [5]_____, where smart devices monitor patients at home. Based on the data received, [6]_____, or medications could be delivered by drones. Crime may be reduced by [7]_____ which would alert police of possible crimes.

「…してもいいですか」と相手に許可を求める際、英語では以下のような表現を使うことができます。

☐ **Can [May] I ...?** (…してもいいですか) ※ May I ...? の方が丁寧な表現。

　例 **Can I** ask you a question? (質問をしてもいいですか)

☐ **Is it OK if I ...?** (…してもいいですか) ※許可されるかどうか分からない状況

　例 **Is it OK if I** stay overnight at Tom's house? (トムの家に泊まってもいいですか)

☐ **Do you mind if I ...?** (…しても差し支えありませんか)

　例 **Do you mind if I** visit you this afternoon? (今日の午後、伺っても差し支えありませんか)

　　※ Do you mind if I ...? は、相手が嫌がるかもしれないと気持ちを推し量るニュアンス

☐ **答え方**

　例 Is it OK if I ask you a question? (質問してもいいですか)

　　— **Sure. What would you like to know?** (もちろんです。何をお知りになりたいですか)

　　— **Of course. Go ahead.** (もちろんです。どうぞ)

　例 Do you mind if I ask you a question? (質問してもよろしいですか)

　　— **No, not at all.** (もちろんです) / **Sure. What it is?** (もちろんです。何でしょうか)

Speak Out

次の **A** と **B** に取り組み、都市と科学技術についての会話をしましょう。

A　学習した表現を使って、次の会話文を完成させましょう。完成後、ペアで練習しましょう。
　　　_____ には、**Tips for Speaking** の表現が入ります。

A: _____ a question?

B: Sure. _____?

A: Do you think it's good for cities to have so many smart cameras?　I mean, they're everywhere these days.

B: Yes, because _____.

A: But what about the privacy of citizens?

B: Well, in my opinion, _____.

B 次の質問についてパートナーと会話をしましょう。必要に応じて、**Useful Vocabulary and Expressions** の表現を使ってみましょう。

1. Imagine what cities might look like in 50 years. What is your image?

> Me

> My Partner

2. What technology would you like to see in cities which would make them more efficient?

> Me

> My Partner

Useful Vocabulary and Expressions

- digitalization （デジタル化）
- sustainable （持続可能な）
- privacy （プライバシー）
- regional city （地方都市）
- personal information （個人情報）
- ICT (information and communication technology) （情報コミュニケーション技術）
- monitor （監視する）
- artificial intelligence （人工知能：AI）
- take measures against cyber crimes （サイバー犯罪への対策を行う）
- increase contact between citizens and government （市民と政府の接点を増やす）
- solve urban problems （都市問題を解決する）

8 Historical Sites

Talk with Your Partner

次の質問についてペアで会話をしましょう。

Q1 Can you name three old buildings or structures* in your country?
*structure 建築物

A _____

Q2 Can you name three old buildings or structures in other countries?

A _____

Listen to the Dialogue

Helen のイタリア旅行についての会話を聞き、次の A ～ C に取り組みましょう。

A 会話を聞き、写真の内容が話の順番になるよう、1 ～ 4 の番号を記入しましょう。 23

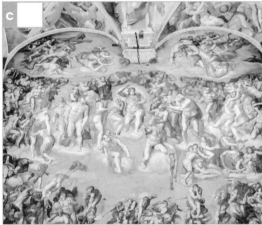

B 会話の内容について、最も適切な語 (句) の記号を **a.** ～ **c.** の中から1つずつ選びましょう。

1. A person who throws money into the Trevi Fountain will (a. have good luck
   b. return to Rome someday   c. live a long life).

2. The Sistine Chapel* is located in (a. Rome   b. Venice   c. Vatican City).
   *chapel 礼拝堂

3. It took Michelangelo (a. 4   b. 6   c. 8) years to paint the ceiling of the
   Sistine Chapel.

67

M: Hi, Helen. How was your trip to Italy?

W: Great! Let me show you some ¹_____. This is the Colosseum in Rome. It was built in the first ²_____ for entertainment, performances and sports.

M: Wow, it's ³_____, isn't it? … What are you doing in this photo?

W: I'm throwing a ⁴_____ into the Trevi Fountain of Rome. Everyone does it. It means that you will one day ⁵_____ to the city.

M: That's interesting. … Oh, I know what this photo is. It's the ⁶_____ of the Sistine Chapel in Vatican City. It was painted by Michelangelo.

W: Yes. He started painting it in 1508. But it was very ⁷_____ work and took him four years to ⁸_____. … And you know what this photo is.

M: Of course. It's the Leaning Tower of Pisa. Did you ⁹_____ to the top?

W: Yes, all 294 ¹⁰_____! Now let me show you some pictures of Venice.

Tips for Listening	固有名詞の発音・アクセントに注意して聞こう

人名や地名といった固有名詞の中には、日本語と英語で発音が異なるものが多く含まれます。発音やアクセントの位置などに注意して聞きましょう。Holland ／オランダや Vienna ／ウィーンのように全く似ていないものもあるので注意しましょう。

Task 次の英語を日本語にしましょう。その後、音声を聞いてリピートしましょう。 🎧 24

1. Munich 都市名 ___ミュンヘン___   2. Aristotle 人名 _____

3. Moscow 都市名 _____   4. van Gogh 人名 _____

5. Greece 国名 _____   6. Bach 人名 _____

7. Vatican City 国名 _____   8. Michelangelo 人名 _____

Grammar Preview　受動態

The Old Man and the Sea **was written** by Ernest Hemingway.（『老人と海』はヘミングウェイによって書かれました）のように、動作を受ける物や人を主語として焦点化し、「〜が…される」という意味を表す表現形式を**受動態**《be 動詞＋動詞の過去分詞形》と呼びます。《by ＋ 行為者》は必要がある場合にのみ示し、行為者が不明だったり言及する必要がなかったりする場合は示しません。

Task 日本語に合うように、空欄に適切な語句を入れましょう。

1. 滋賀県の延暦寺は 788 年に建立されました。

   Enryakuji Temple in Shiga Prefecture _____.

2. 私のスマホにはそのアプリはインストールされていません。

   That app _____.

3. レポートは英語で書かれなければいけません。

   Your essay must _____.

Vocabulary Preview

語群の中から適切な語句を選び、**1.** 〜 **6.** の空欄に入れましょう。

> precisely（正確に）　limestone（石灰岩）　tomb（墓）
> afterlife（死後の世界）　mummy（ミイラ）　robber（泥棒）

1. John dressed up as an Egyptian _____ for Halloween.

2. People of many religions believe in an _____.

3. Follow the directions _____ and your cake will taste delicious.

4. _____ was often used as a building material.

5. The _____ stole two bags of money from the bank.

6. The _____ contained some fine gold jewelry and Roman coins.

ピラミッドに関する **Short Talk** を聞き、次の **A** ～ **C** に取り組みましょう。

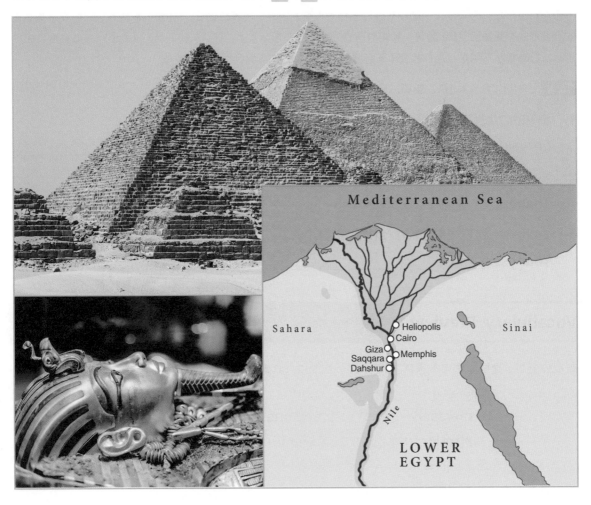

A **Short Talk** を聞き、内容に合うものを **a.** ～ **c.** の中から１つずつ選びましょう。 25

1. How long did it take to build the Great Pyramid of Giza?

   a. About 20 years   b. About 46 years   c. More than 100 years

2. Where were the bodies of Egyptian kings usually placed?

   a. Near the top of pyramids

   b. In the center of pyramids

   c. Underneath pyramids

B 空欄に入る適切な語 (句) を入れて **Short Talk** の内容をまとめましょう。

Recap

The Great Pyramid of Giza

- The pyramid dates back to King Khufu about ¹_____ years ago.
- It was built with more than two million huge blocks of ²_____ carried by boat across ³_____ and from southern areas.
- To give the pyramid its smooth appearance, exterior blocks of ⁴_____ were cut very ⁵_____.

Pyramids as tombs

- Egyptian kings believed in life after death, and their bodies were carefully ⁶_____ for their afterlives.
- After a king died, the ⁷_____ was usually placed underground inside a pyramid, along with food and other necessities.
- The inner passages were hidden and blocked to protect them against ⁸_____.

C 以下を参考にしながら、**Short Talk** の内容のリテリングをしましょう。

Retell

※空欄に記入する必要はありません

The Great Pyramid of Giza dates back ¹_____. Over a period of ²_____, more than two million huge blocks of stone ³_____ across the Nile River and from southern areas. Exterior blocks of white limestone were cut very precisely to give the pyramid ⁴_____.

The pyramids are actually ⁵_____. Egyptian kings believed in ⁶_____. After a king died, the body was ⁷_____. It was usual to ⁸_____, along with ⁹_____. The inner passages of the pyramids were hidden and blocked to ¹⁰_____.

「驚き」の感情を示したい時には次のような表現を使うことができます。

☐ **驚いたことをストレートに表現する**

That's unbelievable [incredible / amazing]! (信じられない)
I can't believe it! (信じられない)
What a surprise! (それは驚いた)

☐ **間投詞（「えぇ！」という驚きを表す）**

Oh! / Wow! / What!? / Gee! / Oh, dear!　※ oh, dear は通例、よくないことに対して用いる。

☐ **相手に尋ねる**

Really? / Seriously? / Are you sure? (本当？)
Isn't it surprising [amazing]? (すごいと思わない？)

☐ **その他**

No kidding! / No way! (そんなわけないよ)
I didn't know that! (それは知らなかったよ)

Speak Out

次の **A** と **B** に取り組み、歴史的な名所についての会話をしましょう。

A 学習した表現を使って、次の会話文を完成させましょう。完成後、ペアで練習しましょう。
＿＿＿＿＿＿ には、**Tips for Speaking** の表現が入ります。

A: Did you go anywhere during the holidays?

B: Yes, I went to ＿＿＿＿＿＿＿＿＿＿＿＿＿＿＿＿＿＿＿＿＿＿＿＿＿.

A: ＿＿＿＿＿＿＿＿＿＿＿＿ Tell me about it.

B: Well, it ＿＿＿＿＿＿＿＿＿＿＿＿＿＿＿＿＿＿＿＿＿＿＿.

　　And ＿＿＿＿＿＿＿＿＿＿＿＿＿＿＿＿＿＿＿＿＿＿＿＿.

A: ＿＿＿＿＿＿＿＿＿＿＿＿ I'd like to go there someday, too.

B 次の質問についてパートナーと会話をしましょう。必要に応じて、**Useful Vocabulary and Expressions** の表現を使ってみましょう。

1. Why do people like to visit old buildings and structures?

> **Me**
>
>
>

> **My Partner**
>
>
>

2. Is it important to preserve historical buildings and structures?
   Why or why not?

> **Me**
>
>
>

> **My Partner**
>
>
>

Useful Vocabulary and Expressions

- cathedral （大聖堂）
- temple （寺）
- shrine （神社）
- national park （国立公園）
- palace （宮殿）
- ancient remains （遺跡）
- historic district （歴史のある地区）
- a must-visit place （絶対に行くべき場所）
- a magnificent building （荘厳な建物）
- a spectacular view （壮観な景色）
- was built [established] by ... in ~ （…によって~年に建てられた）
- was registered as a World Heritage Site in ... （…年に世界遺産に登録された）
- be worth seeing [visiting] （見る［訪れる］価値がある）
- attract many tourists all over the world （世界中から多くの観光客をひき寄せる）

Unit
9 Sports & the Brain

Talk with Your Partner

次の質問についてペアで会話をしましょう。

Q1 What sports did you enjoy playing when you were younger?

A _____

Q2 How often do you exercise or play sports?

A _____

74

Listen to the Dialogue

Clark さんと医師の会話を聞き、次の **A**〜**C** に取り組みましょう。

A 会話を聞き、イラストの内容が話の順番になるよう、1〜4の番号を記入しましょう。

B 会話の内容について、最も適切な語 (句) の記号を **a.**〜**c.** の中から1つずつ選びましょう。

1. Ms. Clark has been doing aerobics (**a.** since she was a child   **b.** since high school   **c.** since she began working).

2. The doctor doesn't think it's good to exercise (**a.** before breakfast   **b.** after lunch   **c.** late at night).

3. The doctor recommends (**a.** taking short naps* during the day   **b.** exercising outside   **c.** drinking milk before bed).   *nap 昼寝

75

M: Hello, Ms. Clark. What seems to be the problem?

W: I'm not sleeping well, doctor. It takes me ¹_____ to fall asleep at night.

M: I see. Do you ²_____ regularly or play any sports?

W: Yes. After I started working, I also started doing aerobics for about 30 minutes every night. I thought it would give me more ³_____.

M: Aerobics is great, but that's actually the ⁴_____ time to exercise. You see, when you exercise, your ⁵_____ rate and body temperature increase, and it takes time to return to ⁶_____. That may be why you're not falling asleep ⁷_____. You're probably ⁸_____ during the day, too, right?

W: That's right. In fact, I sometimes fall asleep at my desk.

M: Try exercising outside before going to work. The natural ⁹_____ will help you sleep better at night. I think you'll feel more ¹⁰_____ during the day, too.

Tips for Listening　　複数形の -s の発音に注意して聞こう

名詞の複数形には、/s/ /z/ /ɪz/ の３通りの発音があります。
　① books /s/　　　② legs /z/　　　③ glasses /ɪz/
発音は、-(e)s の直前に来る子音の性質によって変わります。名詞を覚える際にセットで確認しましょう。

Task 音声を聞いて、太字が /s/ /z/ /ɪz/ のどれかを選び○で囲みましょう。その後、音声を聞いてリピートしましょう。　　27

1. brains　　/s/ /z/ /ɪz/　　　　2. athletes　　/s/ /z/ /ɪz/

3. classes　　/s/ /z/ /ɪz/　　　　4. emotions　　/s/ /z/ /ɪz/

5. sports　　/s/ /z/ /ɪz/　　　　6. benches　　/s/ /z/ /ɪz/

7. benefits　　/s/ /z/ /ɪz/　　　　8. muscles　　/s/ /z/ /ɪz/

Grammar Preview 関係代名詞 that

that には、関係代名詞として直前の名詞（先行詞）に情報を加える働きがあります。

例 I'm looking for a tablet computer **that** is light and robust.

（軽くて頑丈なタブレット PC を探しています）

The book (**that**) I had wanted to buy was sold out. (私は買いたかった本は売り切れでした)

The people (**that**) I met in the U.K. were all kind to me.

（私がイギリスで会った人はみんな親切でした）

※ 2、3 文目のように、目的語の働きをする関係代名詞 that は省略されることが多い。

Task 日本語に合うように、空欄に適切な語句を入れましょう。

1. 私が一番好きなスポーツはバスケットボールです。

_____ is basketball.

2 私はポケットがたくさんあるバッグを買いたいです。

I want to buy _____.

3. 私たちが先週観た映画は素晴らしかったです。

_____ was awesome.

Vocabulary Preview

語群の中から適切な語句を選び、**1.** ~ **6.** の空欄に入れましょう。

> eliminate (取り除く)   mood (気分・ムード)   hormone (ホルモン)
> organ (臓器)   activate (作動させる)   benefit (利点)

1. One _____ of studying abroad is experiencing a different culture.

2. The largest _____ in the body is the liver.

3. Any movement will _____ this sensor light.

4. He's always in a good _____ after his favorite team wins.

5. The _____ called insulin* controls the amount of sugar in the blood.
   *insulin インシュリン

6. Credit cards _____ the need to carry large amounts of cash.

スポーツの利点に関する **Short Talk** を聞き、次の A ～ C に取り組みましょう。

A **Short Talk** を聞き、内容に合うものを a. ～ c. の中から1つずつ選びましょう。 28

1. What is one benefit of sports and exercise that is not mentioned?

   a. It helps us control our weight.

   b. It gives us more energy.

   c. It allows us to sleep better.

2. How does exercise help balance our emotional state?

   a. It releases hormones that take away negative feelings.

   b. It makes us focus on other things.

   c. It improves our concentration.

B 空欄に適切な語 (句) を入れて **Short Talk** の内容をまとめましょう。

Recap

- ●Our image of the benefits of sports and exercise
  - *ex.* maintaining a ¹_____ weight, having more energy
  - ➡ Most people don't consider the benefits that physical activity can have on the ²_____ .
  - ➡ Research shows that many athletes and people who exercise ³_____ over a long period of time have healthier brains than non-physically active people.
- ●Benefits of sports and exercise
  - (1) ⁴_____ the brain and allow us to focus and concentrate better
    - ➡ increase our ⁵_____ and improve our ability to learn
  - (2) help to ⁶_____ our mood
    - ➡ Our body releases ⁷_____ that assist in eliminating stress, worry and other negative feelings and emotions.
- ●In short, playing sports and exercising make our brain ⁸_____ better.

C 以下を参考にしながら、**Short Talk** の内容のリテリングをしましょう。

Retell　※空欄に記入する必要はありません

When we think about the benefits of sports and exercise, we usually think of ¹�_____ , having more energy, and building stronger muscles and a healthier heart. One thing that most people don't consider are ²_____ . In fact, research shows that many athletes and people who exercise regularly over a long period of time have ³_____ .

Exercise activates the brain and allows us to ⁴_____ . This increases our productivity and ⁵_____ . Sports and other forms of physical activity also help to ⁶_____ . When we exercise, our body releases hormones that ⁷_____ . In short, playing sports and exercising make our brain work better.

話の内容をまとめたり、要約したりする時は、以下のような表現を使うことができます。日常会話だけでなく、プレゼンテーション等でも使えます。

☐ **in short**（つまり）

例 As we have seen, Eiichi Shibusawa was involved in establishing many companies we know today. **In short**, he is known as the" father of capitalism in modern Japan."（これまで見てきたように、渋沢栄一は今日私たちが知っている多くの企業の設立に関わりました。つまり、彼は「近代の日本における資本主義の父」だったのです）

☐ **to sum up / to summarize / in summary**（まとめると）

例 In today's class, we have learned the seventeen SDGs. **To sum up**, they are the goals that we need to achieve in order to make our planet and life sustainable.（今日の授業では、SDGs の 17 の目標について学びました。まとめると、それらは私たちの地球と生活を持続可能なものにするために達成すべき目標です）

☐ **the point is (that) ...**（ポイントは…）

例 I think we had such a wonderful discussion about the new project. Please remember—**the point is that** we need to consider customers' needs first.（新しいプロジェクトについて素晴らしい議論ができたと思います。ポイントは消費者のニーズを第一に考えることだということを覚えておいてください）

Speak Out

次の **A** と **B** に取り組み、スポーツや健康についての会話をしましょう。

A 学習した表現を使って、次の会話文を完成させましょう。完成後、ペアで練習しましょう。＿＿＿＿＿には、**Tips for Speaking** の表現が入ります。

A: I heard you joined a fitness center. What did your instructor tell you?

B: Well, ＿＿＿＿＿＿, he told me to do everything on this list every time I come.

A: Let me see. ... Oh, he wants you to stretch for 15 minutes, do ＿＿＿＿ sit-ups, ＿＿＿＿＿＿, ＿＿＿＿＿＿ and ＿＿＿＿＿＿. How long does it take to do all that?

B: ＿＿＿＿＿＿＿＿＿＿＿＿.

B 次の質問についてパートナーと会話をしましょう。必要に応じて、**Useful Vocabulary and Expressions** の表現を使ってみましょう。

1. Do you think students should be required to take physical education classes at university? Why or why not?

Me

My Partner

2. Do you consider yourself to be a healthy person? Explain your answer.

Me

My Partner

Useful Vocabulary and Expressions

- do warm-up exercises (準備運動をする)
- work out (筋トレをする)
- do sit-ups (腹筋運動をする)
- swim laps (プールを何往復か泳ぐこと)
- go on a diet (ダイエットをする) / be on a diet (ダイエット中である)
- go to the gym to get in shape (健康のためにジムへ行く)
- be out of shape (運動不足である)
- jog around the track ... times (運動場を…周走る)
- gain about 10 kilograms (10 キロほど太る)

- do aerobic exercises (有酸素運動をする)
- do push-ups (腕立て伏せをする)
- ride an exercise bike (フィットネスバイクに乗る)
- lift weights (ウエイトトレーニングをする)

Unit
10 Poetic Justice

Talk with Your Partner

次の質問についてペアで会話をしましょう。

Q1 Do you consider yourself to be a lucky person? Why or why not?

A _____

Q2 Can you name a hero in a book, movie or manga? Why is he/she a hero?

A _____

Listen to the Dialogue

Amanda と友人の会話を聞き、次の A ～ C に取り組みましょう。

A 会話を聞き、イラストの内容が話の順番になるよう、1 ～ 4 の番号を記入しましょう。 29

B 会話の内容について、最も適切な語 (句) の記号を a. ～ c. の中から 1 つずつ選びましょう。

1. Amanda went to a theme park with her (a. friend   b. sister   c. cousin).

2. The two women (a. shared a car with two handsome guys   b. enjoyed the view from the Ferris wheel*   c. didn't get on the Ferris wheel).
   *Ferris wheel 観覧車

3. It took (a. two   b. ten   c. twenty) minutes to fix the Ferris wheel.

83

C もう一度会話を聞き、空欄に入る語を記入しましょう。

29

M: Hi, Amanda. Did you and your cousin enjoy ¹_____ at the theme park?

W: Yes. But there were a ²_____ of people who didn't have fun.

M: What happened? Did they have an ³_____?

W: Not ⁴_____. We were getting ready to get on the Ferris wheel. Then all of a sudden two guys cut in ⁵_____ and got in the car.

M: That wasn't very nice. Did you get in the same car as them?

W: No, we ⁶_____ to wait and get in the next car ..., which was a good thing.

M: Why? Did you ⁷_____ with a couple of handsome guys?

W: No-o-o! We didn't even get on the Ferris wheel. A few seconds later, it stopped suddenly, and ⁸_____ could get off. But luckily, it only took 10 minutes to fix.

M: Well, I ⁹_____ you and your cousin had the last laugh, then.

W: Yeah! Ha ha ha! ... Oh, I took a ¹⁰_____ of those two guys. Look.

Notes   have the last laugh 最後に笑う car ゴンドラ

Tips for Listening　　冠詞の発音に注意して聞こう

英語の冠詞 (a、an、the) は、会話等ではそれぞれ弱く発音されます。a は /ə/、an は /ən/、the は /ðə/ にそれぞれなります (the は次に来る単語が母音で始まる時に /ði/ になります)。冠詞を強調したい場合は、それぞれ /eɪ/ /æn/ /ðíː/ と発音されます。

Task 音声を聞いて空欄に入る語句を書きましょう。その後、音声を聞いてリピートしましょう。

30

1. I think _____ _____ great idea!

2. I want you to get some bananas and _____ _____.

3. My father usually goes to _____ _____ at eight a.m.

4. _____ _____ difference between a violin and a viola?

Grammar Preview 前置詞＋関係代名詞

That is the house **in which** he lived when he was young.（あれは彼が若い頃に住んでいた家です）
という文では、the house という名詞に対して in which 以降が情報を加える役割を果たしています。こ
のように、《前置詞＋関係代名詞》を使って名詞を後ろから修飾することができます。前置詞には、in 以外
にも on や to、with といったものが使われます。なお、That is the house **which** he lived **in** when he
was young. のように、前置詞を後ろに移動することも可能です。

Task 《in ＋関係代名詞》を使い、日本語に合うように空欄に適切な語句を入れましょう。

1. 横浜は、私が生まれた市です。

    Yokohama is the city _____ .

2. 1914 年は、第一次世界大戦（World War I）が始まった年です。

    1914 is _____ .

3. 昨夜私は、雲の上を飛んでいる夢を見ました。

    Last night I had a dream _____ .

Vocabulary Preview

語群の中から適切な語句を選び、**1. ～ 6.** の空欄に入れましょう。

bribe（賄賂）	deserve（…に値する）	arrest（逮捕する）
reward（[努力等に応じて] …に報いる）	punish（罰する）	justice（正義）

1. The police came to _____ the man for causing the accident.

2. He has a good sense of _____ and fairness.

3. You can _____ children for good behavior in many different ways.

4. The company decided not to _____ the worker for his mistake.

5. An honest person will never take a _____ .

6. After all your hard work, you _____ a holiday.

因果応報に関する **Short Talk** を聞き、次の **A** ～ **C** に取り組みましょう。

A   **Short Talk** を聞き、内容に合うものを **a.** ～ **c.** の中から 1 つずつ選びましょう。   31

1. What is poetic justice?

   a. The idea that there are more good people than bad people in the world

   b. The idea that people are not always treated fairly

   c. The idea that goodness is rewarded and badness is punished

2. According to the example in the talk, why does the government worker deserve his punishment?

   a. He stole some money.   b. He took a bribe.   c. He lied to a judge.

B 空欄に適切な語 (句) を入れて **Short Talk** の内容をまとめましょう。

Recap

● Poetic justice in movies and books
 - *Frozen*: Queen Elsa saves her kingdom.
  ⇔ Hans, the man who tried to kill her and become king, is ¹_____ and sent back to his homeland.
 - *The Harry Potter* series: Harry ²_____ the evil Voldemort.
  ⇔ Hogwarts School is again able to safely ³_____ its young students.
● poetic justice ＝ a form of justice in which good ⁴_____ are rewarded and bad ⁵_____ is punished
● Instances of poetic justice in our everyday lives
 Ex. 1: An excellent, hard-working employee receives a large ⁶_____.
 Ex. 2: A government worker goes to prison for accepting ⁷_____.
 ➡ In the first case, the employee deserves his ⁸_____, while in the second case, the government worker deserves his punishment.

C 以下を参考にしながら、**Short Talk** の内容のリテリングをしましょう。

Retell
※空欄に記入する必要はありません

At the end of the Disney animation *Frozen*, Queen Elsa saves her kingdom. Hans, the man who tried to kill her and become king, is ¹____. In the *Harry Potter* series, Harry defeats the evil Voldemort, and Hogwarts School is again able to ²____. These are two examples of poetic justice, a form of justice in which ³____ and ⁴____.

Poetic justice isn't limited to ⁵____. We see instances of poetic justice all the time in our everyday lives. One example of this would be when an excellent, hard-working employee ⁶____. A government worker who goes to prison for ⁷____ is another example. In the first case, the employee ⁸____, while in the second case, the government worker ⁹____. That's poetic justice.

会話で言葉に詰まった時には次のような表現を使うことができます。

☐ **well ... / umm ... / Let me see. ...** （えー／うーん）

例 A: What do you do in your free time?

B: **Well**, I like karaoke.

☐ **you know ...** （…ですよね）

例 A: Let's go to Hawaii this summer.

B: I'd like to, but we need to consider the cost, **you know**.

☐ **I mean ...** （私が言いたいのは…）

例 A: What do you think of the new project?

B: Well, I don't think we can do it. **I mean**, the schedule is too tight.

Speak Out

次の A と B に取り組み、因果応報についての会話をしましょう。

A 学習した表現を使って、次の会話文を完成させましょう。完成後、ペアで練習しましょう。
_____ には、**Tips for Speaking** の表現が入ります。

A: Can you think of a story in which poetic justice is done? A movie? A fairytale?

B: _____. ... Oh, I know—Cinderella. She's very kind-hearted, but her step-sisters are always mean to her. But in the end, she marries the prince and lives happily ever after. And you? Can you think of a good example?

A: _____ ... how about _____? In that story

_____

_____.

Notes step-sister 義理の姉 live happily ever after いつまでも幸せに暮らしましたとさ

B 次の質問についてパートナーと会話をしましょう。必要に応じて、**Useful Vocabulary and Expressions** の表現を使ってみましょう。

1. Do you believe in the idea of poetic justice? Explain your answer.

> Me

> My Partner

2. Give an example of poetic justice in your life in which you were rewarded for something you did.

> Me

> My Partner

Useful Vocabulary and Expressions

- consequence (結果)
- scenario (シナリオ)
- play (演劇)
- misfortune (不幸)
- theme (テーマ)
- What goes around comes around. (因果応報)
- be dominated by greed (欲望に駆られる)
- undergo hardship (苦難を体験する)
- do a good deed (良い行いをする)

- revenge (復讐)
- novel / story (小説)
- enemy (敵)
- happy ending (ハッピーエンド)
- fate (運命)

- crime (犯罪)
- period drama (時代劇)
- trick (…を騙す)
- eventually (結果的に)

The Magic of Hot Springs

Talk with Your Partner

次の質問についてペアで会話をしましょう。

Q1 Have you ever been to a hot spring? If yes, how many times?

A _____

Q2 Can you name any other countries that are famous for their hot springs?

A _____

Listen to the Dialogue

日本に住んでいる留学生の Susan が冬休みについて友達に話しています。会話を聞き、次の **A** 〜 **C** に取り組みましょう。

A　会話を聞き、イラストの内容が話の順番になるよう、1〜4の番号を記入しましょう。

B　会話の内容について、最も適切な語 (句) の記号を **a.** 〜 **c.** の中から1つずつ選びましょう。

1. Susan went skiing in (**a.** Gifu　**b.** Nagano　**c.** Niigata) Prefecture.

2. According to Susan, the hot spring she went to after skiing was (**a.** crowded **b.** large **c.** relaxing).

3. Susan visited a monkey park on the (**a.** first　**b.** second　**c.** third) day of her trip.

M: Did you do anything [1]_____ during your winter break, Susan?

W: Yes, I went skiing in Nagano Prefecture with a few of my [2]_____.

M: I didn't know you [3]_____ ski.

W: I can't. Actually, I spent most of the time on my [4]_____. Ha ha ha! Anyway, after that, we went to a hot spring, or *onsen* in Japanese. The water was nice and warm, and it was so-o-o [5]_____! That was the best part of my whole trip.

M: That [6]_____ wonderful. I've heard so much about Japanese hot springs.

W: So have the monkeys.

M: What do you [7]_____?

W: Well, on the second day, we visited Jigokudani Monkey Park. It had a hot spring [8]_____ of Japanese monkeys. They had come down from the [9]_____ to warm up. It was really fun [10]_____ them. ... Oh, and we also visited Zenkoji Temple.

Tips for Listening　　/æ/ と /ɑ/ の発音に注意して聞こう

英語には、日本語の「ア」に似た母音が複数あります。その中でも特に、/æ/（例 **a**pple）と /ɑ/（例 h**o**t）に注意が必要です。/æ/ は、長方形をイメージしながら口を横に開き、「エ」と「ア」を素早く連続して発音する感覚です。/ɑ/ は、指が 3 本入るくらい口を縦に大きく開けて発音します。

Task 音声を聞いて、太字が /æ/ か /ɑ/ のどちらかを選び○で囲みましょう。その後、音声を聞いてリピートしましょう。　　33

1. b**o**ttle　　/æ/ /ɑ/　　　　　　2. c**a**p　　　　/æ/ /ɑ/

3. **a**ngry　　/æ/ /ɑ/　　　　　　4. b**o**dy　　　/æ/ /ɑ/

5. c**o**ffee　　/æ/ /ɑ/　　　　　　6. h**o**nest　　/æ/ /ɑ/

7. **a**nswer　　/æ/ /ɑ/　　　　　　8. **a**nimal　　/æ/ /ɑ/

Grammar Preview | 接触節（名詞 + 主語 + 動詞…）

This is the car **I have wanted to buy**. という文では、the car という名詞の後に《主語＋動詞》を含む節が続いており、「私が買いたいと思っていた⇒車」のように名詞を後ろから修飾しています。これを接触節と呼びます。This is the car **that / which** I have wanted to buy. のように目的格の関係代名詞を入れることもできますが、省略されて接触節になることが多いです。英文を読んだり聞いたりする際に、このパターンの修飾関係を正確に掴むようにしましょう。

Task 接触節を使って，日本語に合うように、空欄に適切な語句を入れましょう。

1. 私が尊敬する科学者はアルバート・アインシュタインです。

   _____ is Albert Einstein.

2. 私たちが昨日観た映画は素晴らしかったです。

   _____ was excellent.

3. 日清食品は，1948 年に安藤百福が設立した (establish) 会社です。

   Nisshin Food is _____.

Vocabulary Preview

語群の中から適切な語句を選び、1. ~ 6. の空欄に入れましょう。

> nerves（神経）　　minerals（ミネラル）　　fatigue（疲労）
> hustle and bustle（喧騒）　　relieve（和らげる）　　heal（治る）

1. Drinking water may help to _____ a headache.

2. The doctor said it would take about two weeks for my injury to _____.

3. Do you prefer the quiet lifestyle of the country or the _____ of a busy city?

4. Playing video games for long hours often results in eye _____.

5. The _____ in our body send signals to and from our brain.

6. Like vitamins, _____ are important for the body to grow and stay healthy.

Listen to the Short Talk

温泉に関する **Short Talk** を聞き、次の **A** 〜 **C** に取り組みましょう。

A Short Talk を聞き、内容に合うものを **a.** 〜 **c.** の中から１つずつ選びましょう。 34

1. What is the talk mainly about?

   a. The reasons why Japanese people visit hot springs

   b. The cultural importance of hot springs in Japan

   c. The health benefits of minerals in Japanese hot springs

2. According to the talk, what is a health benefit of water pressure?

   a. It leads to weight loss.

   b. It creates healthy skin.

   c. It helps blood flow.

B 空欄に適切な語（句）を入れて **Short Talk** の内容をまとめましょう。

Recap

● Hot spring bathing for Japanese people

Hot spring bathing is popular not only because it is a major ¹_____ activity, but also because hot springs offer health ²_____.

- reduce physical and mental stress, improve blood flow, relieve pain, ³_____ skin problems

● How?

(1) People can ⁴_____ the hustle and bustle of everyday life.
　➡ helps remove stress and fatigue, and ⁵_____ the body

(2) Being in warm water reduces muscle stress, and the water pressure allows the blood to ⁶_____ more easily. Warm water also ⁷_____ nerves that relax the body.

(3) Hot spring water contains ⁸_____ that help reduce pain and make healthier, smoother skin.

C 以下を参考にしながら、**Short Talk** の内容のリテリングをしましょう。

Retell
※空欄に記入する必要はありません

Hot spring bathing is a ¹[____] in Japan. But that's not the only reason why Japanese people visit hot springs. Many go for the ²[____], as hot spring baths are known to ³[____], improve blood flow, ⁴[____] and heal skin problems.

How do hot springs do all these things? First of all, by visiting a hot spring, people can ⁵[____]. This helps remove stress and fatigue, and ⁶[____]. Secondly, being in warm water reduces ⁷[____], and the water pressure allows ⁸[____]. Warm water also stimulates ⁹[____]. And finally, hot spring water contains ¹⁰[____].

何かのやり方を説明する際、動作を順番に説明することが求められます。英語では、以下のようなパターンを使うことができます。動作の数によって使用する表現は調整します。

☐ **first → second → third → fourth → finally**

例 Let me explain how to make miso soup. **First**, make dashi stock. **Second**, boil the dashi stock and add vegetables and seaweed. **Third**, put some miso into the broth. **Fourth**, add tofu. **Finally**, serve in individual bowls.

(味噌汁の作り方を説明します。最初に、だし汁を作ります。第二に、だし汁を煮て野菜やノリを入れます。第三に、おたまに味噌を入れます。第四に、豆腐を入れます。最後に、お椀によそいます)

☐ **first of all / to start with → next → then → after that → lastly**

例 I'm going to show you how to pray at a Shinto shrine. **First of all**, throw some money into the offering box. **Next**, bow deeply twice. **Then**, clap your hands twice. **After that**, pray quietly. **Lastly**, bow deeply one more time.

(神社での参拝の仕方を教えます。まず、賽銭箱にお金を投げます。次に、2回深くお辞儀をします。そして、2回拍手をします。その後、静かにお祈りをします。最後に、もう一度深くお辞儀をします)

Speak Out

次の **A** と **B** に取り組み、温泉やお風呂についての会話をしましょう。

A 学習した表現を使って、次の会話文を完成させましょう。完成後、ペアで練習しましょう。
＿＿＿＿＿＿ には、**Tips for Speaking** の表現が入ります。

A: You've been to so many different hot springs. Why do you like them so much?

B: Well, I go for three main reasons. ＿＿＿＿＿＿＿, ＿＿＿＿＿＿＿＿＿＿＿＿＿

＿＿＿＿＿＿＿＿. ＿＿＿＿＿＿, ＿＿＿＿＿＿＿＿＿＿＿＿＿＿＿＿＿.

And ＿＿＿＿＿＿, ＿＿＿＿＿＿＿＿＿＿＿＿＿＿＿＿. Actually,

I'm going to one on Sunday with a few friends. Would you like to come?

A: I'd love to! ... But I get dizzy if I stay in hot water for too long.

B: No problem. The water where we're going is ＿＿＿＿＿＿＿＿＿＿＿＿＿.

B 次の質問についてパートナーと会話をしましょう。必要に応じて、**Useful Vocabulary and Expressions** の表現を使ってみましょう。

1. If you were to visit a hot spring with your friends, what would be your three main reasons for going?

> **Me**

> **My Partner**

2. If an overseas visitor asked you how to take a Japanese-style bath, how would you explain?

> **Me**

> **My Partner**

Useful Vocabulary and Expressions

- public bath（銭湯）
- open-air bath（露天風呂）
- sauna（サウナ）
- bath powder（入浴剤）
- changing room（脱衣所）
- water temperature（お湯の温度）
- soap（石鹸）
- shampoo and conditioner（シャンプーとリンス）
- washcloth（身体を洗うタオル）
- hair dryer（ドライヤー）
- Jacuzzi（ジャグジー）
- soak and relax in a hot bath（熱いお風呂に浸かってリラックスする）
- enjoy viewing natural scenery（自然や景色を楽しむ）
- get dizzy after staying in the tub for a long time（長風呂をしてのぼせる）
- take a lukewarm [half-body] bath（ぬるま湯に浸かる［半身浴をする］）

Unit
12 Living with Less

Talk with Your Partner

次の質問についてペアで会話をしましょう。

Q1 How often do you clean up your room?

A _____

Q2 Do you have clothes you never wear or things you never use? What items?

A _____

Listen to the Dialogue

Janet と友人の会話を聞き、次の **A** ～ **C** に取り組みましょう。

A　会話を聞き、イラストの内容が話の順番になるよう、1 ～ 4 の番号を記入しましょう。

B　会話の内容について、最も適切な語 (句) の記号を **a.** ～ **c.** の中から 1 つずつ選びましょう。

1.　Janet lives in (**a.** an apartment　**b.** a house　**c.** a dormitory*).　*dormitory 寮

2.　She will sell (**a.** some　**b.** most　**c.** all) of her old books.

3.　She is throwing away a lot of (**a.** food　**b.** cups　**c.** socks).

C もう一度会話を聞き、空欄に入る語を記入しましょう。

M: What are all these boxes doing in your living room, Janet? Are you
1_____ into a new apartment?

W: No, I finally decided to **2**_____ the place. There are so many things I
don't need or use **3**_____.

M: What are you going to do with **4**_____?

W: I'm going to sell most of my old books. And I'm going to give all the
5_____ that I don't wear anymore to charity. I'm **6**_____ a lot
of old magazines, socks, towels and things like that, too.

M: When you're done, **7**_____ feel like you've moved into a new apartment.

W: Ha ha ha! Yeah. ... Actually, I've **8**_____ finished cleaning up my
bedroom. Come and take a **9**_____.

M: ... Wow! It looks **10**_____ different.

Note charity 寄付

Tips for Listening	接続詞の弱形に注意して聞こう

接続詞の and、or、but には強く読まれる発音（強形）と弱く読まれる発音（弱形）があります。日常会話では、
それらを強調する必要がある場合を除き、後者で発音されることが多いです。

    and: (強) /ænd/ (弱) /ən(d)/   or: (強) /ɔːr/ (弱) /ər/   but: (強) /bʌt/ (弱) /bə(t)/

Task 音声を聞いて空欄に入る語句を書きましょう。その後、音声を聞いてリピートしましょう。　36

1. Would you like _____ _____ _____?

2. _____ _____ _____ us.

3. Sorry, _____ _____ _____ go with you.

Grammar Preview 《同格》を表す that

I agree with the idea **that people should pay for plastic shopping bags**. (私はレジ袋を有料化すべきだという考えに賛成です) という文では、that 節が the idea の内容を表しています。これを《同格の that》と呼びます。このパターンで使われる主な名詞として、idea (考え) や fact (事実)、suggestion (提案)、news (ニュース、知らせ)、opinion (意見)、decision (決定)、hope (希望) などが挙げられます。

Task 日本語に合うように、空欄に適切な語句を入れましょう。

1. 彼が試験に合格したという知らせに驚きました。

   I was surprised by _____.

2. 子どもの数が減少しているという事実に向き合うべきです。

   We should face _____.

3. 小学校で英語を教えるべきだという考えに反対です。

   I'm against _____.

Vocabulary Preview

語群の中から適切な語句を選び、**1. ~ 6.** の空欄に入れましょう。

> clutter (散らかっているもの)   mental (精神的な)
> problematic (問題のある)   minimalist lifestyle (ミニマリスト的な生活様式)
> fulfilling (充実した)   emotional (感情的な)

1. Staying up late every night is _____ for people who must get up early.

2. A _____ means living with only the things you really need.

3. I can never find anything in my room because of all the _____.

4. _____ training often helps athletes perform better.

5. Sam and Brenda became very _____ at their daughter's wedding.

6. Jane enjoyed a _____ career as a nurse.

ミニマリストのライフスタイルに関する **Short Talk** を聞き、次の **A** 〜 **C** に取り組みましょう。

A　**Short Talk** を聞き、内容に合うものを **a.** 〜 **c.** の中から1つずつ選びましょう。　

1. According to the passage, which of the following statements is true?

   a. Most people don't have all the things they need.

   b. Many people believe that happiness can be bought.

   c. Most people only buy things that have a real purpose.

2. What is the main purpose of *danshari*?

   a. To save money

   b. To clean up the house

   c. To bring more joy to one's life

B 空欄に適切な語 (句) を入れて **Short Talk** の内容をまとめましょう。

Recap

The idea of "more is better" and "happiness can be bought"

➡ Most people own many more things than they actually need or use.
   ➡ This is particularly ¹_____ in Japan.
   Why? ➡ Space is often ²_____, and houses and apartments can quickly ³_____ up with things with no real purpose.

Minimalist lifestyle

➡ removing the clutter and living with a ⁴_____ number of things
= *danshari* in Japanese, or decluttering
   ➡ not only ⁵_____ clutter but also ⁶_____ and emotional clutter
   ➡ Through *danshari*, you'll have the space, time and ⁷_____ to live a happier and more ⁸_____ life.

C 以下を参考にしながら、**Short Talk** の内容のリテリングをしましょう。

Retell
※空欄に記入する必要はありません

Modern culture has brought with it the idea that ¹▓▓▓▓▓▓▓▓, and that ²▓▓▓▓▓▓▓▓. As a result, most people own many more things than they actually need or use. This can be problematic in Japan, where ³▓▓▓▓▓▓▓▓.

Recently, more and more people are switching to a minimalist lifestyle by ⁴▓▓▓▓▓▓▓▓, and living with ⁵▓▓▓▓▓▓▓▓. This lifestyle is called *danshari*, and it refers not only to ⁶▓▓▓▓▓▓▓▓. It carries with it the promise that ⁷▓▓▓▓▓▓▓▓. In short, ⁸▓▓▓▓▓▓▓▓.

「…したらどうですか」と相手にある行為をすることを提案する際、英語では以下のような表現を使うことができます。

☐ **Why don't you ...?** (…したらどうですか)

例 **Why don't you** give it a try? (やってみたらどうですか)

☐ **How about ...?** (…はどうですか)

例 **How about** asking for your parents' help? (両親に助けてもらうのはどうですか)

☐ **I think you should ....** (…するべきだと思います)

例 **I think you should** prioritize what you do.

(すべきことに優先順位をつけるべきだと思います)

☐ **I suggest [recommend] (that) you (should) V ....** (…することを提案 [お勧め] します)

例 **I suggest (that) you (should) scan** the documents.

(書類をスキャンしておくことを提案します)

☐ **You might as well ....** (…した方がいいと思いますよ)

例 **You might as well** buy some eggs. (卵を買った方がいいですよ)

Speak Out

次の **A** と **B** に取り組み、ミニマリストのライフスタイルについての会話をしましょう。

A 学習した表現を使って、次の会話文を完成させましょう。完成後、ペアで練習しましょう。
_____ には、**Tips for Speaking** の表現が入ります。

A: Wow! Your apartment is so clean! How do you keep it this way?

B: Well, I _____.

A: My room is full of books, manga, DVDs, old clothes... What should I do?

B: _____?

A: That's a great idea! Do you think you could help me with that?

B: _____.

B 次の質問についてパートナーと会話をしましょう。必要に応じて、**Useful Vocabulary and Expressions** の表現を使ってみましょう。

1. Do you agree with the statement "Living with less is best"? Why or why not?

> **Me**

> **My Partner**

2. Do you agree with the idea that happiness can be bought? Why or why not?

> **Me**

> **My Partner**

Useful Vocabulary and Expressions

- storage space (収納スペース)
- closet (クローゼット)
- underutilized (有効活用されていない)
- second-hand store (リサイクルショップ)
- throw away unnecessary things (不要なものを捨てる)
- decide what to keep (残しておくものを決める)
- take out the garbage (ごみを捨てる)
- buy ... on impulse (…を衝動買いする)

- tidy up (整理する)
- over-stuffed room (物であふれかえる部屋)
- daily routine (日々やること)

Unit
13 Street Food

Talk with Your Partner

次の質問についてペアで会話をしましょう。

Q1 What comes to mind when you think of street food?

A _____

Q2 Do you think it's OK to eat food while walking or while on a train or bus?

A _____

Listen to the Dialogue

Cathy と友人のストリートフードについての会話を聞き、次の **A** ～ **C** に取り組みましょう。

A　会話を聞き、イラストの内容が話の順番になるよう、1～4 の番号を記入しましょう。 38

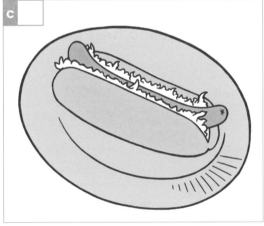

B　会話の内容について、最も適切な語 (句) の記号を **a.** ～ **c.** の中から1つずつ選びましょう。

1. Cathy is worried about (a. food safety　b. the price of food　c. finding a food cart*).　*food cart 屋台

2. There are (a. 500　b. 1,500　c. 5,000) food carts and food trucks in New York.

3. (a. Some　b. Almost all　c. All) food cart owners must have a license*.
   *license 免許

C もう一度会話を聞き、空欄に入る語を記入しましょう。

M: How do you like New York, Cathy?

W: I love it! There are so many [1]_____ things to do and see.

M: Yeah. Hey, how about getting [2]_____ from a food cart and eating in the park?

W: Well, New York is [3]_____ for its food carts, but is the food [4]_____ to eat?

M: I've been eating it for 10 years, and I've never gotten [5]_____. Ha ha ha! But seriously, all of the city's 5,000 food carts and food trucks [6]_____ grades from the New York City Health Department, just like regular [7]_____.

W: Oh, good. So we'll just find [8]_____ that has a grade "A" rating.

M: Almost all of them do, so that won't be a [9]_____. Also, all of the owners must have a [10]_____ and wear it around their neck when they're working.

W: OK. I'm going to have a New York hot dog, then.

M: Me, too. Let's go.

Note rating 評価

Tips for Listening | /t/ の発音に注意して聞こう

better や water が、「ベラー」や「ワーラー」のように聞こえることがあります。これはアメリカ英語に見られる現象で、具体的には、強勢が置かれる音節で /t/ が母音に挟まれると、日本語のラ行（またはダ行）のように発音が変化します。なお、イギリス英語にはこの現象は見られません。

Task 音声を聞いて空欄に語句や文を書きましょう。その後、音声を聞いてリピートしましょう。 39

1. _____ 2. _____ 3. _____

4. _____ 5. _____ 6. _____

7. _____ 8. _____

Grammar Preview | or と名詞の並列による《同格》

同格の関係を表す際、that 以外にも以下のような表現の仕方があります。

(1)《名詞 1》, or《名詞 2》

例 ***Natto*, or fermented beans,** is a traditional Japanese food.

（納豆、つまり発酵した豆は日本の伝統的な食品です）

(2) 名詞を並列させる

例 **Mr. Ellis, our new English teacher,** is from New Zealand.

（私たちの英語教師であるエリス先生はニュージーランド出身です）

Task 日本語に合うように、空欄に適切な語句を入れましょう。

1. 私たちのマネージャーの Bill は、6月に結婚したばかりです。

_____, just got married in June.

2. AI、つまり人口知能（artificial intelligence）は私たちの社会で重要な役割を果たしています。

_____, plays an important role in our society.

3. 有名な日本人野球選手である大谷翔平は、多くの人々に愛されています。

_____,

is loved by many people.

Vocabulary Preview

語群の中から適切な語句を選び、**1.** ～ **6.** の空欄に入れましょう。

shrine（神社）	vendor（[街頭等の] 物売り、露店）	staple（無くてはならないもの）
flavorful（風味豊かな）	portable（持ち運び可能な）	typically（一般的に）

1. The pasta dish contains many _____ spices.

2. I love my tablet computer because it's light and _____.

3. Baseball games _____ take about three hours to play.

4. It's very common in Japan to visit a _____ on New Year's Day.

5. Tim bought this baseball cap from a _____ outside the stadium.

6. Toasters are a _____ in most kitchens.

ストリートフードに関する **Short Talk** を聞き、次の A ～ C に取り組みましょう。

A **Short Talk** を聞き、内容に合うものを a. ～ c. の中から 1 つずつ選びましょう。 40

1. According to the talk, when are food carts usually set up in Japan?

    a. Around lunchtime

    b. In the evening

    c. Late at night

2. How did soba vendors attract customers in 17th century Japan?

    a. They beat on drums.

    b. They blew whistles.

    c. They sang.

B 空欄に適切な語 (句) を入れて **Short Talk** の内容をまとめましょう。

Recap

- Street food is popular throughout the world.
  - → It's fast, flavorful and ¹_____.
- Street food in Japan is often sold from *yatai*.
  - → a type of ²_____ food cart typically selling ramen and other hot foods
  - - usually set up in the evening at various ³_____ and removed late at night or early in the morning
  - - ⁴_____ often stop by *yatai* for a quick meal.
- *Yatai* have been ⁵_____ since the 17th century.
  - - commonly ⁶_____ outside temples and shrines, and known for selling soba
  - - Later, vendors started selling ramen ⁷_____ of soba.
  - - Today, *yatai* have become a ⁸_____ at festivals, offering everything from *yakisoba* and *takoyaki* to *yakitori* and roasted corn.

C 以下を参考にしながら、**Short Talk** の内容のリテリングをしましょう。

Retell ※空欄に記入する必要はありません

Street food is popular throughout the world. It's ¹_____. Street food in Japan is often sold from *yatai*, a type of portable food cart typically selling ²_____. These carts are usually set up ³_____ and removed late at night or early in the morning. Business people often stop by *yatai* for a quick meal after a long day at the office.

Yatai have been around ⁴_____. They were commonly found ⁵_____, and were known for selling soba. Later, vendors started selling ⁶_____. Today, *yatai* have become a staple at festivals.

会話では、自分の言いたいことが相手に十分伝わらないことがあります。その場合、別の表現を使って言い換えることが必要となります。英語では、以下のような表現を使うことができます。

☐ **In other words, ...**（言い換えると）

例 If you want to improve your English skills, output is very important. **In other words**, you need to speak and write in English a lot.

（英語力を上げたいのであれば、アウトプットがとても大切です。 言い換えると、 英語でたくさん話したり書いたりすることが必要です）

☐ **That is to say, ...**（すなわち）**/ To put it a different way, / To put it another way,**（別の言い方をすると）

例 You were absent from this class six times. **That is to say,** you cannot get credits.（あなたはこの授業に 6 回欠席しました。すなわち、単位を修得することはできません）

☐ **What I'm trying to say is ...**（私が言おうとしていることは…）

例 I don't mean to hurt you. **What I'm trying to say is** that you should be humbler.

（君を傷つける気持ちはありません。私が言おうとしていることは、もっと謙虚になるべきということです）

Speak Out

次の A と B に取り組み、ストリートフードや祭りについての会話をしましょう。

A 学習した表現を使って、次の会話文を完成させましょう。完成後、ペアで練習しましょう。
_____ には、**Tips for Speaking** の表現が入ります。

A: You went to a summer festival on the weekend, right? How was it?

B: Oh, it was _____! I had *yakisoba, yakitori, takoyaki, ...*

A: _____, you just ate.

B: Yeah, most of the time. Ha ha ha! But I did a few other things, too.

A: Like what?

B: Well, I _____, _____ and _____.

B 次の質問についてパートナーと会話をしましょう。必要に応じて、**Useful Vocabulary and Expressions** の表現を使ってみましょう。

1. What do you like to do at summer festivals?

Me

My Partner

2. Why do you think street food is so popular is places like New York?

Me

My Partner

Useful Vocabulary and Expressions

- summer festival （夏祭り）
- stall （屋台）
- corn dog （アメリカンホットドッグ）
- lottery stall （くじ引き）
- food truck （キッチンカー）
- festival mask （お祭りのお面）
- stroll around ... （…を歩き回る、散歩する）
- have a lively atmosphere （賑やかな雰囲気である）
- be full of people （人でいっぱいである）
- grab some food （食べ物を買いに行く）

- fireworks display （花火大会）
- cotton candy （綿菓子）
- goldfish scooping （金魚すくい）
- Japanese lantern （提灯）
- ring toss （輪投げ）

14 Going Cashless

Talk with Your Partner

次の質問についてペアで会話をしましょう。

Q1 How much cash do you usually carry with you?

A _____

Q2 Do you make any cashless payments (credit card, train pass, etc.)?

A _____

Listen to the Dialogue

Ed が電話で Beth に助けを求めています。会話を聞き、次の A ～ C に取り組みましょう。

A 会話を聞き、イラストの内容が話の順番になるよう、1 ～ 4 の番号を記入しましょう。

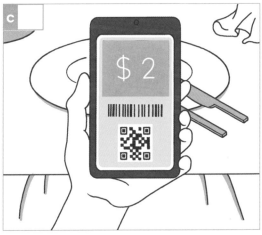

B 会話の内容について、最も適切な語 (句) の記号を **a.** ～ **c.** の中から 1 つずつ選びましょう。

1. When Ed calls Beth, he has (**a.** no money   **b.** $2   **c.** $10) in his e-wallet.

2. Beth's suggestion is for Ed to (**a.** find an ATM   **b.** call his parents   **c.** add money to his digital wallet).

3. Ed will return Beth's money (**a.** tomorrow   **b.** in a few days   **c.** in a week).

もう一度会話を聞き、空欄に入る語を記入しましょう。　🎧 41

M: Sorry for calling late, Beth, but I ¹_____ if you can help me.

W: Sure, Ed. What can I do for you?

M: Well, I just finished having dinner at a restaurant, but I can't pay the ²_____. I don't have any ³_____, and there's only $2 in my e-wallet.

W: Then why don't you just ⁴_____ money from your bank account?

M: I ⁵_____ if I could, but ...

W: ...but you don't have any money in your account, ⁶_____.

M: Right. I ⁷_____ almost everything on textbooks and school ⁸_____ this week.

W: OK, wait a ⁹_____—I'm sending you some money now. ... Did you get it?

M: ... YES! Thanks, Beth. I'll pay you ¹⁰_____ tomorrow. I work part-time at a supermarket, and tomorrow is payday.

Notes　bank account 銀行口座　payday 給料日

Tips for Listening　　脱落に注意して聞こう①

/p/ /b/ /t/ /d/ /k/ /g/ は、破裂音と呼ばれる子音です。英語には、破裂音が連続する時に最初の音が発音されなくなるという現象があります。これを脱落（elision）と呼びます。例えば、Not too bad. では、/nɑt/ /tuː/ のように /t/ が連続しますが、最初の /t/ は発音されず、「ナットゥーバッ」のように聞こえます。

Task　音声を聞いて空欄に入る語句を書きましょう。その後、音声を聞いてリピートしましょう。　🎧 42

1. Please _____ _____ of yourself.

2. It was such a _____ _____!

3. _____ _____ around and get on with your work!

4. He looked sick yesterday, _____ _____ he looks fine.

Grammar Preview　助動詞＋完了形（**have** ＋動詞の過去分詞形）

Q. He **would be** 70 years old. と He **would have been** 70 years old. はどのように違うでしょうか。

前者が「今、彼は 70 歳になっているでしょう」に対して、「（過去の時点で）彼は 70 歳になっていたでしょう」という意味を表します。過去を振り返って「…していただろう」「…だったに違いない」といった推量を表す際は、《助動詞＋完了形》の形を用います。助動詞には、would、must、may [might]、can't [couldn't]、could、 should [ought to] 等が用いられるので、状況に応じて使い分けることが必要です。

Task 日本語に合うように、空欄に適切な語句を入れましょう。

1. 私はその時彼女に本当のことを伝えるべきでした。

   I _____ then.

2. 彼はホテルに帰る途中で道に迷ったのかもしれません。

   He _____ on his way to the hotel.

3. ベスは間違った電車に乗ったに違いありません。

   Beth _____ the wrong train.

Vocabulary Preview

語群の中から適切な語句を選び、1. ～ 6. の空欄に入れましょう。

> hacker (ハッカー)　　　shift (転換)　　　drawback (欠点)
> withdraw ([お金を] おろす)　advantage (利点)　simplicity (単純さ)

1. He has the _____ of a good education.

2. The _____ of the design makes the machine easy to build.

3. I must _____ some money from my bank account today.

4. The main _____ of this apartment is its small size.

5. This site was attacked by a _____ last night.

6. The government recently announced a _____ in policy.

キャッシュレス社会に関する **Short Talk** を聞き、次の **A** 〜 **C** に取り組みましょう。

A　**Short Talk** を聞き、内容に合うものを **a.** 〜 **c.** の中から1つずつ選びましょう。

1.　According to the talk, what are the biggest advantages of going cashless?

　　a. Safety and security　b. Cost and savings　c. Simplicity and convenience

2.　What is the speaker suggesting at the end of the talk?

　　a. The disadvantages of a cashless society outweigh* the advantages.

　　b. The trend towards a cashless society will probably continue.

　　c. People should have a choice between cash and electronic payments.
　　　*outweigh …よりまさる

B 空欄に適切な語（句）を入れて **Short Talk** の内容をまとめましょう。

Recap

- Not too long ago, the idea of a cashless society would have sounded like science fiction.
  → Today, many countries are moving in this ¹_____.
- The biggest advantages → ²_____ and ³_____
  - tapping your phone on an electronic payment machine
  - sending e-money to family or friends with a few ⁴_____ on your phone
  - no need to visit a ⁵_____ bank or look for an ATM to withdraw cash
- A few drawbacks
  - Electronic payments aren't as private as cash payments.
  - The ⁶_____ risk → Hackers are always out there trying to steal money.
  - Technology failures could prevent people from accessing their ⁷_____.
- The global ⁸_____ towards a cashless society is unlikely to stop.

C 以下を参考にしながら、**Short Talk** の内容のリテリングをしましょう。

Retell
※空欄に記入する必要はありません

Not too long ago, the idea of a cashless society would have ¹_____. But today, many countries are ²_____. The biggest advantages are ³_____. What could be easier than ⁴_____ on an electronic payment machine, or sending e-money to family or friends with ⁵_____? There's no need to ⁶_____ or ⁷_____.

All this sounds wonderful, but there are ⁸_____. Electronic payments aren't ⁹_____. Personal information could ¹⁰_____. There is also ¹¹_____. In addition, technology failures could prevent people ¹²_____. Despite these concerns, the global shift towards a cashless society is ¹³_____.

あるテーマについて賛成や反対の意見を述べる際、以下のような表現を使うことができます。

☐ 《賛成》を表す

I agree (with you). （賛成です）　※以下のような副詞を組み込むことで程度を調整することが可能。

I totally / completely [partially] agree (with you). （完全に［部分的に］賛成です）

I agree in principle. （大筋では賛成です）

I think you're right. （その通りだと思います）

That's true. （確かにそうです）

You're absolutely right. （まさにその通りです）

☐ 《反対》を表す

I'm afraid I don't agree. （賛成ではありません）

I can't agree with you on that point. （その点については賛成できません）

I'm not sure I can agree with you. （賛成できかねます）

I'm against ... （…に反対です）

I have a different point of view on that. （その点について別の見方をもっています）

That's an interesting point, but I don't agree. （それは興味深いですが、私は反対です）

Speak Out

次の A と B に取り組み、キャッシュレス社会についての会話をしましょう。

A 学習した表現を使って、次の会話文を完成させましょう。完成後、ペアで練習しましょう。
_____ には、**Tips for Speaking** の表現が入ります。

A: You know, when you think about it, cash is pretty dirty, isn't it? I mean, nobody washes it, so it must be full of germs* and things. 　*germ 菌

B: _____. I think we should go 100% cashless.

A: _____. It would be difficult for a lot of older

people because _____.

B: _____.

B 次の質問についてパートナーと会話をしましょう。必要に応じて、**Useful Vocabulary and Expressions** の表現を使ってみましょう。

1. Do you think Japan will one day become a cashless society? (Explain your answer.)

> Me

> My Partner

2. Do you think the advantages of going cashless outweigh the disadvantages? (Explain your answer.)

> Me

> My Partner

Useful Vocabulary and Expressions

- banknote (紙幣)
- cash payment (現金支払い)
- self-checkout (セルフレジ)
- receipt (レシート)
- bank transfer (銀行振り込み)
- financial transaction (金融取引)
- settlement fee (決済手数料)
- prepaid card (プリペイドカード)
- purchase [order] history (購入履歴)
- PIN (number) (暗証番号)
- hold one's smartphone over the QR code (QR コードにスマホをかざす)
- use a credit card from a company with a good point return rate
  (ポイント還元率の高い会社のクレジットカードを使う)
- top up one's card (カードにチャージする)

Unit 15 English as a Global Language

Talk with Your Partner

次の質問についてペアで会話をしましょう。

Q1 Can you name six English-speaking countries?

A _____

Q2 Which English-speaking country would you like to visit? Why?

A _____

Listen to the Dialogue

外国からの夫婦が日本人女性に話しかけています。会話を聞き、次の **A** ～ **C** に取り組みましょう。

A 会話を聞き、イラストの内容が話の順番になるよう、1～4の番号を記入しましょう。

B 会話の内容について、最も適切な語（句）の記号を **a.** ～ **c.** の中から1つずつ選びましょう。

1. The couple left their (a. English map　b. guidebook　c. dictionary) in their hotel room.

2. The couple wants to go to (a. Akasaka　b. Akihabara　c. Asakusa).

3. The young woman will (a. take the couple to a subway station　b. give the couple directions to a station　c. buy tickets for the couple).

C もう一度会話を聞き、空欄に入る語を記入しましょう。

M: Excuse me, miss. Do you speak English?

W: ... A little. ... Do you need some ¹_____?

M: Yes, my wife and I forgot our English ²_____ in our hotel room, and we're a little ³_____. She has a map, but it's all in Japanese.

W: OK. ... Umm ... ⁴_____ do you want to go?

M: Well, we read that Asakusa is an interesting place to ⁵_____, so we thought we'd check it ⁶_____ today.

W: Asakusa! Yes, it's a very popular ⁷_____ of Tokyo. I think you'll like it. You can get there by ⁸_____ in about 20 minutes. Let me take you to the ⁹_____, and then you can buy your tickets.

M: OK, thank you very much. That's very kind of you.

W: Not at all. It's my ¹⁰_____.

Note Not at all. とんでもないです

Tips for Listening 〉 脱落に注意して聞こう②

「脱落に注意して聞こう①」では、Take care. (/téɪk/ /kéər/) のように、同じ音が連続した時の脱落を見ました。これ以外にも、破裂音 (/p/ /t/ /d/ /k/ /g/) の後に摩擦音 (例 /s/ /ʃ/ /θ/ /f/ /v/) や /l/ /m/ /n/ が来た時に、前者が脱落することがあります。

Task 音声を聞いて空欄に入る語句を書きましょう。その後、音声を聞いてリピートしましょう。 45

1. Would you _____ _____, please?

2. We had such a _____ _____ in Okinawa.

3. He left home _____ _____.

4. I think the man was wearing a _____ _____.

Grammar Preview   過去分詞の形容詞的用法

English is a language **spoken all over the world**. という文では、過去分詞で始まる spoken all over the world が、前にある a language という名詞に対して情報を加えています。このように過去分詞を使うと、「…されている（された）」という意味を名詞に付け加えることができます。例文では、「英語＝話されている」という関係です。なお、English is a language **widely** spoken all over the world. のように、名詞と過去分詞の間に副詞（句）が入ることもあるので注意が必要です。

Task 日本語に合うように、下線部に適切な語句を入れましょう。

1. 私はドイツ製の腕時計を買いたいです。

    I want to buy _____.

2. 彼は日本と韓国の多くの若者によって愛されている歌手です。

    He is _____ in Japan and South Korea.

3. あれは有名なフランス人建築家（architect）によってデザインされた建物です。

    That is _____.

Vocabulary Preview

語群の中から適切な語句を選び、**1. ～ 6.** の空欄に入れましょう。

> fluency（流暢さ） promotion（昇進） worldwide（世界中に［で］）
> transfer（異動） rewarding（やりがいのある） official language（公用語）

1. The airline flies to more than 200 cities _____ .

2. The _____ of Brazil is Portuguese.

3. She speaks both Japanese and English with great _____ .

4. Donna received a _____ to Sales Manager on June 1.

5. The company offered her a _____ to the London office.

6. James finds his work as a volunteer very _____ .

国際語としての英語に関する **Short Talk** を聞き、次の **A** 〜 **C** に取り組みましょう。

A   **Short Talk** を聞き、内容に合うものを **a.** 〜 **c.** の中から１つずつ選びましょう。 46

1. Which of the following sentences is not true?

    a. There are 1.5 billion native English speakers worldwide.

    b. English is an official language in over 50 countries.

    c. As a foreign language, English is taught more than any other language.

2. According to the talk, what is true about English websites?

    a. Fifty percent of the most visited sites are in English.

    b. About sixty-seven percent are American sites.

    c. Eighty percent of the sites are viewed by non-native speakers.

B 空欄に適切な語（句）を入れて **Short Talk** の内容をまとめましょう。

Recap

- English as a "global language"
  - about 1.5 ¹_____ English speakers worldwide, including 400 million native speakers
  - an ²_____ language in more than 50 countries
  - the language most often taught as a ³_____ language
  - the language most commonly used for communication between ⁴_____ English speakers
- Situations in which English is either necessary or useful
  - international business ➡ can lead to higher ⁵_____ and promotions, business trips and job ⁶_____ to other countries
  - entertainment *ex*. Hollywood movies, YouTube ⁷_____
  - international travel ➡ easier, more enjoyable and more culturally ⁸_____

C 以下を参考にしながら、**Short Talk** の内容のリテリングをしましょう。

Retell

※空欄に記入する必要はありません

Because English is so widely used globally, it is known as a "global language." Today, there are about ¹_____, including 400 million native speakers. English is an official language in ²_____, and, as a foreign language, it is the one most often taught. It is also the language most commonly used for ³_____.

There are many situations in which English is either necessary or useful. For example, English is the language of ⁴_____. English fluency can lead to ⁵_____. Many of the ⁶_____ are in English, including ⁷_____. Two-thirds of YouTube content and half of the most visited websites are in English. And even a basic level of English makes international travel ⁸_____.

ある話題について相手の意見を尋ねる時には、次のような表現を使うことができます。

☐ **What do you think about this plan?** （この計画についてどう思いますか）

☐ **What's your opinion of this problem?** （この問題についてあなたの意見はどうですか）

☐ **How do you feel about it?** （それについてどう思いますか）

☐ **Do you have any ideas [suggestions]?** （何かアイデア［提案］はありますか）

☐ **Is there anything you want to add?** （何か付け加えたいことはありますか）

☐ **Where do you stand on this proposal?** （この提案についてどういう立場ですか）

☐ **What are your thoughts on this project?** （このプロジェクトについてどう思いますか）

☐ **I'd love to hear what you think.** （ぜひあなたの意見を聞かせてください）

Speak Out

次の **A** と **B** に取り組み、英語学習やホームステイについての会話をしましょう。

A 学習した表現を使って、次の会話文を完成させましょう。完成後、ペアで練習しましょう。
_____ には、**Tips for Speaking** の表現が入ります。

A: I want to go to Canada for two months this summer on a homestay, but my parents think I should work and save my money. _____?

B: In my opinion, _____ because
_____.

A: OK, thanks. I'll think about what you said. _____?

B: Yes, I also think you should _____.

B 次の質問についてパートナーと会話をしましょう。必要に応じて、**Useful Vocabulary and Expressions** の表現を使ってみましょう。

1. People often say that Japanese worry too much about making mistakes when they speak English. What are your thoughts on this?

Me

My Partner

2. For you, what's the most difficult English skill to learn—reading, writing, listening or speaking? Why?

Me

My Partner

Useful Vocabulary and Expressions

- pronunciation (発音)
- accent (アクセント)
- intonation (イントネーション)
- dialect (方言)
- native speaker (母語話者)
- foreign language (外国語)
- first language (母語)
- variety (変種)
- inter-cultural communication (異文化間コミュニケーション)
- English proficieny test (英語力テスト)
- put Japanese into English (日本語を英語にする)
- worry too much about making mistakes (ミスを犯すことを過度に心配する)
- memorize new vocabulary (新出単語を覚える)
- enhance mutual understanding (相互理解を促進する)

クラス用音声CD有り（別売）

English Echo
—Advancing Listening Proficiency with Inspiring Topics
時代に合ったトピックで強化するリスニングスキル

2023年2月20日　初版発行

著　者　Robert Hickling / 森本 俊

発行者　松村達生

発行所　センゲージ ラーニング株式会社

〒102-0073　東京都千代田区九段北1-11-11　第2フナトビル5階
電話 03-3511-4392
FAX 03-3511-4391
e-mail: eltjapan@cengage.com
copyright © 2023 センゲージ ラーニング株式会社

装丁・組版　　藤原志麻（クリエイド・ラーニング株式会社）
編集協力　　　クリエイド・ラーニング株式会社
本文イラスト　増渕芽久美
印刷・製本　　株式会社エデュプレス

ISBN 978-4-86312-404-2